Beyond Baked Beans

BUDGET

BUDGET FOOD FOR STUDENTS

Absolute Press

Fiona Beckett

Beyond Baked Beans BUDGET

BUDGET FOOD FOR STUDENTS

First published in Great Britain in 2006
by **Absolute Press**
Scarborough House
29 James Street West
Bath BA1 2BT
Phone 44 (0) 1225 316013
Fax 44 (0) 1225 445836
E-mail info@absolutepress.co.uk
Website www.absolutepress.co.uk

Reprinted 2007.

© Fiona Beckett, 2006

Publisher Jon Croft
Editor Meg Avent
Publishing Assistant Meg Devenish
Designer Matt Inwood
Illustrator Andy Pedler

A catalogue record of this book is available
from the British Library

ISBN 9781904573456

Printed and bound by Printer Trento, Italy

For more information visit
www.beyondbakedbeans.com

FOR IMPOVERISHED STUDENTS EVERYWHERE...

CONTENTS

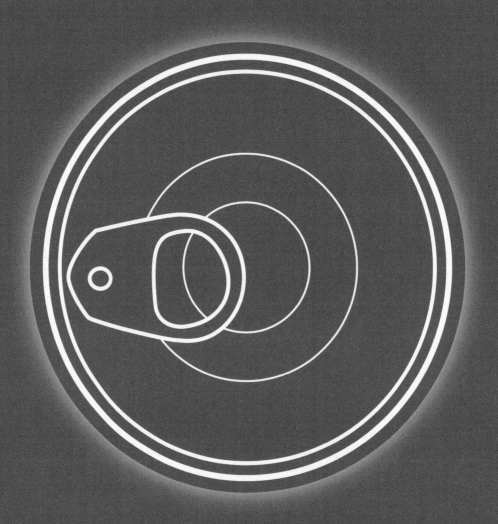

CHEAP CAN BE HEALTHY

Let's face it cheap food has a bad press. Justly so. Think of the ingredients and meals you currently buy and eat and chances are they're far too high in sugar, fat and salt. But hundreds of thousands of people all over the world manage to feed their families healthily on what you have to spend in a week. It can be done. Not only that, it can be fun.

To achieve it you have to learn two things – how to cook, obviously, but equally important how to shop. Not only what to buy but what to do with it. This is undoubtedly more difficult if you're catering primarily for yourself which is why this latest book in the *Beyond Baked Beans* series focuses particularly on shopping and cooking for one – and what to do with the leftovers. Hence the title of the first section – **SURVIVE**.

The middle section, **SHARE**, is for those occasions when you do have to cook for a crowd but still want to keep costs down. Quite a few of the recipes are veggie, not only because they're cheap and healthy but also because it makes it easier to cater for veggies and non-veggies alike. But I hope you'll like the new spins on that perennial student favourite bolognese.

Lastly **SPOIL YOURSELF** is exactly that. Some indulgent but not over-indulgent recipes. It's a myth to think that to be a treat, food must necessarily be fattening (although anxious chocolate lovers can go straight to p136)

Eating cheaply and well is above all a question of attitude; of wanting to play the bargain-hunting game; of believing that cooking is a skill worth acquiring. That eating together is sociable and civilised, wasting food is profligate and that feeling energetic and healthy is preferable to feeling perpetually wrecked. Bit of a no-brainer, isn't it?

8 HOW TO SURVIVE ON A BUDGET

Figures differ but the average UK student currently spends around £20-28 a week on food depending on whether the calculations involve eating out. That's just under £3 to £4 a day... quite tight if you're catering for yourself, not at all bad if you're living in a student house and pooling your resources. However it's all too easy as we all well know to blow the lot in one supermarket visit and not have a lot to show for it. The only answer is to learn to shop – and eat – cannily so that you really make your money work for you. Bye bye impulse shopping, hello bargain hunting....

HOW TO BUDGET – THE 10 GOLDEN RULES

1 PLAN YOUR SHOPPING TRIP

If you really want to stick to a budget you need to make a plan. Not a totally inflexible one (you still need to be in a position to snap up a particularly good bargain) but at least have an idea before you go out of what you're going to cook. Take a look at these recipes to see what appeals to you, then make a list, taking care you don't duplicate ingredients you already have. If you're buying just for yourself, rather than a household, the key thing is to make every thing you buy earn its keep. Just look, for example, at how far you can stretch a single chicken (pp48–53) or how to get every last gram out of a block of cheese (pp74–75).

2 SHOP TWICE A WEEK

Don't plan too far ahead. If you try to plan a whole week's meals, chances are you'll waste at least some of the food you've bought. I find it better to plan in 3- to 4-day blocks, which also enables you to ring the changes, varying what you eat so you don't get bored. If you've decided to have three meals based on mince you might well want to switch to stir-fries or noodles, for example.

3 SCRIMP AT THE START OF THE WEEK

Try and leave yourself enough money each week to give yourself a treat, perhaps a bottle of olive oil, a lump of parmesan or a large bar of chocolate. If you eat frugally at the beginning of the week it's more likely you can splash out at the end. That's also the time to take advantage of special offers on things you eat regularly like bacon, pasta and tuna.

4 BUY THINGS AS YOU NEED THEM

Obviously you'll have to make an initial outlay on some basic stores, but don't go mad and buy a whole lot of stuff you may not need (unless your parents are paying of course...). Many ingredients can be substituted. For example, if you want an onion flavour, you can use onions, spring onions or leeks. If you want to make a dish hotter, you could use paprika, chilli powder, fresh chillies or chilli sauce.

5   LEARN WHAT THINGS COST...

That might sound an impossible task given the several hundred lines in the average supermarket, but you should at least know the price of the things you buy regularly, like pasta, tinned tomatoes or cheese so that alarm bells ring if you find them at a higher price than you usually pay or, conversely, at a knock-down price. Remember though a bargain isn't a bargain if you don't, or can't, use it before it goes off.

6   ...AND WHAT'S IN SEASON

If you insist on buying strawberries in January or leeks in June, you'll pay for them. Food that's in season tastes better too. For a list of what's in season when see p17. Sometimes retailers sell produce at a high price even when it's in season though. I've been shopping for root veg in winter and found parsnips at four times the price of carrots. You need to keep your wits about you.

7   AVOID CONVENIENCE FOODS

Well obviously not completely. I don't expect you to make your own mayonnaise, and most of us use pre-packed stir-fry veg. But do you really need to buy ready-grated cheese? Unwrapped fruit and veg also tend to be substantially cheaper than pre-packed and you only need buy the amount you're going to use (see p17).

8   DON'T SCOFF THE LEFTOVERS!

Behave as if you're on a diet, serve up what you're going to eat (which can be quite substantial – I'm not advocating diet rations), cool the rest down, wrap it up and put it in the fridge. OK, I know we all pick at leftovers and conduct fridge raids in the early hours, but if you really want to save money you can't afford to eat next day's food.

9   SAVE ON FUEL

It's cheaper to cook on top of the stove than it is in the oven. If you do use the oven try to cook more than one thing – a tray of roast peppers that could be used for sandwiches and salads for example (p64), while you're cooking a roast.

10   BE MORE ADVENTUROUS!

The more types of food you're prepared to eat, the cheaper your shopping basket will be. Experiment with own-brand versions of the foods you like. Give cheap, nutritious foods like liver and sardines a try. (Not at the same time, obviously.)

10 THE GREAT PROTEIN MYTH

One of the things that stops us thinking creatively about budget food is our over-reliance on protein, especially animal based protein. For many people a meal is not a meal without a substantial hunk of meat. But that may mean you're locked into a way of eating you can't really afford and which isn't particularly well-balanced.

According to student adviser and nutritionist Kerry Torrens – who provides the nutritional advice on my website www.beyondbakedbeans.com – most students eat too much protein. She advises that a nineteen year old woman should be eating 45g of protein a day. The National Diet and Nutrition Survey of 2004 reports that young women of that age group actually eat 59.9g – about 33% more. And a moderately active nineteen year old male needs 55.5g of protein but will more likely be consuming 77.8g, about 40% more than he needs.

It's easier to grasp how little you need if you relate the figures to individual foods. A relatively small 150g chicken breast, for example, provides 42g of protein, just under a young woman's minimum daily requirement. Add a glass of semi-skimmed milk (7g) and she would have reached her target. A male student who eats a modest portion of spaghetti bolognese made with 100g of lean mince (32g) topped with cheddar (6g) and a helping of baked beans on wholemeal toast (16g), plus milk in his tea and coffee would meet his daily requirement too. Other cheap sources of protein are eggs (7-8g, depending on the size), tuna (25g per 100g portion) and pulses like red kidney beans and lentils (15g per 200g cooked weight). Even bread and peanut butter contain some protein (6g for 2 slices of wholemeal bread, 4.5g for a tablespoon of peanut butter). It just goes to show that you don't have to rely solely on meat to get the protein you need.

GETTING YOUR VITS

The other thing it's easy to overlook when you're trying to cut costs is getting enough vitamins and minerals. Torrens points out that students who drink and smoke need to boost their vitamin C intake (cheap sources include oranges, kiwi fruit, red peppers and strawberries in season) and vitamin B (contained in fortified breakfast cereals, pork and Marmite and other yeast extracts) which can otherwise get depleted.

Many female students will also be short of calcium that is vital for bone and muscle health, and iron that is particularly important for women because of their monthly blood loss. A deficiency can cause tiredness and listlessness. Calcium can be found cheaply in dairy products like milk, cheese, yoghurt and fromage frais, and in oily fish like mackerel and sardines. Iron is found in significant quantities in red meat, nuts, lentils and other pulses, green leafy vegetables, fortified breakfast cereals and wholemeal bread.

CHEAP SUPERFOODS

Here's a list of healthy but inexpensive food that may not be part of your current diet but which you should try and eat as often as possible because of the range of nutrients they provide:

Broccoli, carrots, cabbage;
Sprouts and dark leafy greens like spinach and watercress;
Red peppers, tomatoes (fresh or tinned), garlic;
Oranges, kiwi fruit, strawberries, apples, bananas;
Sardines, brazil nuts, peanuts (provided you're not allergic to them, obviously);
Sunflower seeds and porridge oats

12 HOW TO BAG A BARGAIN

WHERE TO SHOP

You might assume – as most people do – that the only place to shop cheaply is the supermarket. This is not strictly true. Of course they often have some good bargains (see below) but they balance these by charging more for other items. Obviously I'm not advocating that you trek round every shop in the neighbourhood comparing prices, simply that you should be aware what different kinds of food shops might have to offer. Don't make assumptions that certain kinds of shops such as independent butchers are expensive.

SUPERMARKETS

Supermarkets are highly sophisticated shopping environments. From the time you walk in through the luscious fresh produce of the fruit and veg department to the time you check out everything is designed to grab your attention.

They cater primarily for people who are cash-rich and time-poor – not you in other words. They make their money out of adding value to products – washing and pre-packing them so that you don't have to do the work. But you obviously pay for the convenience.

Next time you go to a supermarket take a look at the price of loose carrots. Next, check how much it costs to buy them pre-packed (the unit cost, i.e. price per kilo or 100g, is given on almost all products). Chances are that they will cost at least twice as much.

They also, as you'll have noticed, have several different quality levels. Ranges like 'Finest' (Tesco) and 'Taste the Difference' (Sainsbury's) at the top of the tree, 'Basics' or 'Value' at the bottom. These budget ranges are the ones you should try. (These products are often stacked right at the bottom of the shelf rather than at eye level by the way.)

Ingredients also tend to be expensive if they're in demand. Products like chicken breasts, rump steak, salmon fillets, salads, popular cheeses like Mozzarella, Feta and Mascarpone – the sort of ingredients you find on TV cookery programmes – are generally pricier than their less sexy equivalents (chicken thighs, minute steak, loose lettuces, English regional cheeses, Quark and curd cheese). The same applies to the products you might need for making fashionable Asian dishes like coriander, soy sauce and fish sauce. But there can be good offers on these sort of lines at particular times of year when supermarkets want to lure customers away from their competitors – Christmas, Valentine's Day and Chinese New Year, for example.

Then there's the infamous BOGOF (buy one get one free) which can sound incredibly tempting but would you buy it if it didn't have that sticker on it? And 3 for the price of 2 may not be a good offer at all if it encourages you to buy something you can't or won't use by the eat-by date. What I look out for are special offers on products I use regularly and will keep for at least a couple of weeks like bacon, tuna or pasta.

Another good buy in supermarkets is fresh produce that's reduced. That can be any day of the week but there are usually some good offers available at the beginning of the week on produce that hasn't sold over the weekend. Some of my best bargains have been bagged at the supermarket at my local petrol station which often reduces lines by up to 80% on a Sunday evening. You need to use them up quickly though – the reason they're cheap is that they've reached their sell-by date.

The best way to use supermarkets is for basics. They're hard to beat for everyday items like tea, coffee, cooking oil, pasta and breakfast cereals for tinned products like tomatoes, tuna and beans, particularly if you use own brands. And veggies may find certain products like honey and vegetable bouillon powder cheaper than in a health food shop (though not products like nuts and dried fruits – see p15).

DISCOUNT STORES
e.g. Aldi, Lidl and Netto

The new generation of discount supermarkets are cheap, no doubt about it, but they do have a few drawbacks. The range of products they carry is typically not as wide as the average supermarket and the quality of fresh produce, particularly meat and fish isn't as good. You may also face unexpected charges for car parking or carrier bags (not much, admittedly). The big supermarkets have also responded to the competition they pose by increasing the items in their budget ranges so on many products they're not that much cheaper. But you do tend to find the odd really good bargain – recent finds have been very cheap bread products like naan and pitta bread and excellent German-style sausages (Aldi and Lidl are both German-owned). Worth checking out if you have one near you certainly, though don't expect to find everything you want in there.

14 HOW TO BAG A BARGAIN

INDEPENDENT FOOD SHOPS

The general perception is that small specialist shops are really expensive. Some, such as smart urban delis, are certainly going to be beyond your reach. But others, such as old-fashioned butchers and fish shops can provide really cheap food.

SPECIALIST SHOPS

e.g. butchers, fishmongers, greengrocers, bakers

A dying breed, but there are still some great examples left. What they excel at is the sort of produce that supermarkets won't touch (less expensive cuts of meat, in the case of butchers, less common types of fish or locally grown fruit and veg). Get to know the people behind the counter and you may even get great advice too on what to buy and how to cook it. A good baker is a real find; decent bread is hard to find in supermarkets.

'ETHNIC' SHOPS

Great bargains to be found here, especially if you're after particular types of ingredients:

Indian/Pakistani/Bangladeshi grocers – spices, cheap pulses, fresh herbs like mint and coriander.
Greek/Turkish/Middle-Eastern grocers
Wonderful cheap herbs and veg, inexpensive lemon juice, hummus.
Chinese/Asian supermarkets
Cheap soy sauce, fish sauce, sweet chilli sauce, hoisin sauce, rice vinegar, lemon grass, chillies, lime leaves. The only place to shop for a Thai curry.
Afro-Caribbean shops
Good cheap veg.

HEALTH FOOD SHOPS/CO-OPERATIVES

The best place to buy nuts and dried fruits and specialist products like miso or tofu. Can also be good value for beans and other pulses but tend to be expensive for fresh produce which can also be variable in quality if the store does not have a regular turnover.

CORNER SHOPS

Convenient if you've just tumbled out of bed on a Sunday afternoon, but rarely cheap.

CAMPUS SUPERMARKETS

Treat as a corner shop – handy if you're desperate, but certainly not the cheapest place to do the bulk of your food shopping.

MARKETS

If you actually want to enjoy, rather than endure, your food shopping go to a local market. It's likely to be the cheapest place to buy your fruit and veg – so long as you don't get carried away. The big temptation is to buy more than you need, especially towards the end of the day when stallholders are trying to flog what they've got left. If you're just shopping for yourself you do need to ask yourself what you're going to do with 2 kilos of bananas even if you got them for a quid. Produce that may be worth snapping up are foods you can keep for a bit, like onions or other root veg, or ones you can cook in bulk like fresh tomatoes or peppers (if you can be bothered to do that). You may also find specialist stalls selling meat, fish, bread, health foods, or Asian stalls selling good cheap ingredients (see 'Ethnic shops', p14). Farmers' markets are also hugely enticing but tend to be less cheap.

ON-LINE SHOPPING

Much better established than it was even a couple of years ago when my first *Beyond Baked Beans* book was published and a good option for your weekly supermarket shop if you're a) buying for a student house and b) haven't got a car. If you're very well organised you could even band together with neighbours and split the cost of delivery. (That's certainly a good option with veg boxes.) The downside? It's easy to order more than you need, or forget items and then have to shop for them, ending up buying other things you don't really need. Result – a big food bill. (A useful tip though: guilt-ridden parents can sometimes be induced to put through an order for you if you sound as if you're on the verge of starvation, particularly in the first year....)

16 HOW TO BAG A BARGAIN

What you buy obviously reflects what you like and what you plan to cook. But there are bargains to be found in every food category if you only look.

MEAT

Price depends on the cut, but in general you pay more for beef and lamb and less for pork, chicken and turkey. Meat is, however, occasionally affected by health scares so you can find the price of beef or chicken for example suddenly plummets if people stop buying it. (You may not want to buy it either though.)

BEST BUYS

PORK Belly pork (see p59), pork chops, pork mince (often cheaper than beef mince), pork joints. Sausages are almost always on special offer somewhere these days so you should be able to afford at least the middle of the range, rather than the cheapest ones that tend to have very low meat content. I'd always take up a good bacon offer because it keeps well. Streaky is cheaper than back bacon and not too fatty if you fry it till crisp. Packs of ham and cold roast pork are usually well priced too.

CHICKEN Some of the cheapest protein available, but as with eggs there are welfare issues. Personally I'd stick to British. Legs and thighs are generally cheaper than breasts or breast fillets, unless you find a good special offer and have a freezer to store what you don't immediately need.

TURKEY Sometimes cheaper than chicken and can be used for the same sort of recipes. Turkey drumsticks are extraordinarily cheap but somehow extraordinarily unappealing....

BEEF Generally expensive but there are cheap cuts like braising steak and mince. Watch out for prices though on 'extra-lean' mince which are often inflated. Buy cheaper mince, fry it and pour off the fat (see p42). Tinned corned beef is a good buy too.

FISH

Fish really is a brilliant brain food. Best buys include: tinned fish such as tuna, sardines and mackerel, smoked mackerel, frozen fish fillets (see p56) and, if reduced, fresh and smoked salmon and frozen prawns (see p124)

CHEESE

Most cheese is good value if you don't eat too much of it. Trouble is most cheese lovers can't stop nibbling! English regional cheeses like Caerphilly, Cheshire, Red Leicester and Wensleydale are underrated and can be cheaper than Cheddar. Strong cheeses are better value than milder ones because you need less of them for flavour (well, that's the theory anyway!).

BEST BUYS Brie, Cheddar (especially when on special offer), English regional cheeses (see above), Quark (a very good German low-fat cheese), cottage cheese, fromage frais.

OTHER DAIRY PRODUCTS

Go for butter rather than an oil-based spread – the flavour's so much better and it's good for cooking. It's worth paying the little bit extra for spreadable butter – you actually end up using less.

BEST BUYS Large cartons of plain low-fat yoghurt can be used for sweet and savoury dishes. Double cream – a real bargain. Use in savoury sauces or pour over fruit.

EGGS

Cheap and nutritious, so well worth paying the small amount extra it costs to have the hens reared humanely. Buy free-range, please.

FRUIT AND VEG

In theory they should always be cheaper in season (see below) though that isn't invariably the case. They certainly taste better in season though. Try to buy loose rather than pre-packed and don't overlook frozen and canned veg. Frozen peas, peppers and spinach and tinned tomatoes are particularly good value.

BEST BUYS IN WINTER Root veg, especially potatoes, onions and carrots, cabbage and other greens, cauliflower, leeks, citrus fruit (oranges, grapefruit and lemons), apples, pears.

BEST BUYS IN SUMMER Lettuce, cucumber, spring onions, tomatoes, peppers, aubergines, courgettes, strawberries, raspberries, melon, grapes and fresh herbs.

BREAD AND CEREALS

It's worth picking up reduced loaves at the end of the day, particularly if you have a freezer. They taste much better than pre-packed white sliced bread and, if wholemeal, are better for you too. Fortified breakfast cereals and porridge are also a cheap and effective way of getting key vitamins and minerals (see p82).

BEST BUYS Wholemeal pitta bread, naan, crumpets, baguettes or French 'sticks' (much cheaper than Italian ciabatta), own-brand fortified breakfast cereals, porridge. Crispbreads and oatcakes are good for snacks.

SPREADS

Being on a budget you're likely to eat a lot of bread and toast. You need something to liven it up. My choices would be Marmite, peanut butter and clear honey, all of which can be used for other recipes: Marmite for gravy (see p93) peanut butter for salad dressings and dips and honey as a healthier substitute for sugar.

18 STORECUPBOARD BASICS

No student cupboard should be without the following, but buy them only as and when you need them.

COOKING OIL
You can either go for just one type – sunflower oil is the most versatile – or a cheap vegetable oil for frying and an olive oil for salads. Up to you.

PASTA
Italian brands like Buitoni are best if you find them on special offer otherwise stick to own brand, especially spaghetti – regularly half the price of most pasta shapes.

BASMATI RICE
Not the cheapest but it has by far the best flavour. Asian shops have the best prices.

BEANS
Baked, if you like them but borlotti, cannellini and red kidney beans are more versatile, as are chickpeas.

TINNED TOMATOES
The basis of many pasta sauces and stews.

PORRIDGE OATS
Cheap and sustaining (see p82).

SPICES AND FLAVOURINGS
If you haven't got a lot of money to spend on food you need a basic stock of spices and other seasonings to bump up the flavour. Here's what I wouldn't be without.

WINE VINEGAR
Good for salad dressings but also a useful replacement for wine in sauces and stews.

LEMON JUICE
I prefer the taste of fresh lemon but those little squirty bottles last longer. Greek or Cypriot lemon juice has the best flavour.

SALT
Sea salt is nicer than table salt.

PEPPER
Ideally whole peppercorns in a grinder but they are pricey. Most supermarkets now stock a reasonably decent coarse ground black pepper.

GARLIC
Fresh garlic is cheaper or buy a garlic paste from an Asian grocer if you don't like handling it.

DRIED OREGANO AND/OR THYME
The cheapest, most flexible dried herbs without that strong dried herb taste. Or Herbes de Provence but not cheap mixed dried herbs.

PAPRIKA
Useful for jazzing up pasta sauces and stews. Spanish pimenton is the best.

MILD CHILLI POWDER
Useful for chilli (obviously) and zipping up other dishes.

CURRY PASTE
Better than most cheap curry powders and cheaper than cook-in sauces.

TOMATO PASTE
The cheapest way of adding intense tomato flavour, especially to sauces made with fresh tomato. Tubes keep better than jars.

TOMATO KETCHUP
A useful addition to stews and gravies – sweetens and rounds out the flavour.

LIGHT SOY SAUCE
Buy it from a Chinese or Asian supermarket. No need to buy stir-fry sauces.

ORGANIC VEGETABLE BOUILLON POWDER (E.G. MARIGOLD)
Well worth the investment to get a good, natural tasting stock.

PICKLED CUCUMBERS/SWEET PICKLE/PICCALILLI
To jazz up sandwiches, cold meats and cheese.

MY MUST-HAVE MOROCCAN SPICE MIX

As you have to buy four different spices to make this it might seem extravagant but they will make enough to last you a whole year.

Mix up in small batches: 2 tablespoons each of ground coriander and cumin, 1 tablespoon of turmeric and 1–2 teaspoons of chilli powder, depending how hot you like it. A teaspoon or two is brilliant added to a simple tomato sauce (see p37) with veggie stews or with fish.

20 CHEAP KITCHEN KIT

Obviously you can't cook without a few basics but I suggest you buy the majority of your kitchen kit as and when you need it or when you spot a bargain. There are many good sources. Most supermarkets have cheap basic ranges these days, as do high street shops such as Woolworths and Robert Dyas. Ikea is good – if you can face the queues. And so are charity shops, especially for plates, glasses and cutlery.

MUST-HAVES

A KETTLE AND A TOASTER
If not provided by your hall or landlord.

LARGE (PREFERABLY NON-STICK) FRYING PAN
For fry-ups, great for quick meat and fish cooking too. If it's deep enough, it can also double as a wok for stir-frying.

LARGE LIDDED SAUCEPAN OR STEAMER
A pan for pasta and for making large batches of soup. Steamers have an inbuilt colander – ideal for straining pasta when you've finished cooking it. You can also steam veggies and fish.

SMALL/MEDIUM NON-STICK PAN
For scrambling eggs, heating up soup, making sauces, boiling eggs...

LARGE ROASTING DISH
For Sunday lunches and oven baking.

MEDIUM-SIZED MICROWAVEABLE DISH
Obviously essential if you have a microwave, but also fine for conventional ovens. Suitable for crumbles or something like a macaroni cheese.

CHOPPING BOARD
Plastic is easier to clean – and cheaper – so I'd go for that.

SMALL KNIFE FOR PREPARING VEGETABLES, LARGE KNIFE FOR CUTTING/CARVING MEAT
And try and keep them sharp!

A WOODEN SPOON
Preferably two.

LARGE AND SMALL MIXING BOWLS
A large one will double as a salad bowl; the small one is ideal for mixing up salad dressings (though a jam jar is good too), beating eggs, etc.

MEASURING JUG AND SPOONS
Not expensive and will help you follow recipes.

PLUS... A PAIR OF KITCHEN SCISSORS, A CAN OPENER, A FISH SLICE OR SPATULA, A GRATER.

WOULD COME IN USEFUL

WOK
Better than a frying pan for stir-fries. Can also be used as a large saucepan.

HAND-HELD BLENDER
Great for whizzing up soups, dips and spreads.

VEGETABLE PEELER
Not essential but it does make the job easier.

HAND-HELD POTATO MASHER
Ditto. Worth getting if you're heavily into mash.

GARLIC CRUSHER
Quicker and less smelly than chopping by hand.

COLANDER AND/OR SIEVE
Either for draining pasta and rice. A sieve to eradicate lumpy sauces (not that yours will be, of course!).

METAL TONGS
Useful for turning sausages, bits of chicken, etc.

KITCHEN SCALES
Depending how precisely you like to measure things

PLUS... AN ICE TRAY, A BAKING SHEET, A LEMON SQUEEZER, A SERRATED BREAD KNIFE, A ROTARY WHISK (TO WHIP CREAM OR EGG WHITES).

THINK ABOUT A FREEZER!

If you're living in a student house you may want to think about getting a freezer. There are regularly good buys on fresh produce such as meat, fish and vegetables that you can only take advantage of if you have the ability to freeze what you don't immediately need. No need to buy a new one: there are usually plenty in the small ads.

OTHER KITCHEN BASICS

FOIL, CLING FILM, KITCHEN TOWEL, PLASTIC BAGS AND BOXES FOR STORAGE, OVEN GLOVES, APRON, PLASTERS (for when you inevitably cut yourself), FIRE BLANKET OR EXTINGUISHER (just in case...), WASHING-UP LIQUID, SCOURERS/WASHING-UP BRUSH, TEA-TOWELS (enough to always have a clean one), SPONGE CLOTHS, KITCHEN CLEANER, BRILLO PADS (for stuck-on gunk, but no good for non-stick pans), BIN BAGS, FRIDGE THERMOMETER (to tell if your fridge is cold enough; obviously, turn it up if it isn't).

And for the table... FORKS, KNIVES, SPOONS, TEASPOONS, SERVING SPOONS, LARGE PLATES, SIDE PLATES, MUGS (vast quantities of), EGG CUPS, SOUP/CEREAL BOWLS, AND A COUPLE OF SERVING PLATES/BOWLS.

22 HOW TO MAKE FOOD STRETCH

CHANGE THE WAY YOU THINK

Planning what you eat is key to saving cash, particularly if you're shopping for one. It makes it a great deal less likely that you'll have to chuck food out unused and also results in a healthier, more well balanced diet. It does require a change in mindset though, from thinking not just about the next meal but the next few days eating.

Of course I realise the student lifestyle doesn't lend itself to meticulous planning. Some days you need to be up early. Others you can lie in. Often plans will change at the last minute. You go out instead of eating in hall, or at home. You get back late. Others come for a meal. No different to the rest of us really.

But the likelihood is that you will have at least two meals at some point during the day, one of which is likely to be a main meal and one a lighter meal. You also don't want – at least I assume you don't want – to eat the same thing day after day a) because it's boring and b) because it's better from a health point of view if your diet is as varied as possible.

MAIN MEALS AND BEYOND

The best place to start is with the main meal. Is there something you could make that with a few variations could provide several days' eating? A batch of mince, for example, or a stew or a chicken. The second question to ask yourself is, if there is anything you add to the main meal that might create the base for a meal for the following day – like a tin of beans or some rice? Such an advanced degree of forethought may sound daunting but once you get into the habit of asking yourself 'What else can I make with this?' it becomes second nature.

On the following few pages, I've put together a sample few days to start you off. I find it better, as I've mentioned, to plan in blocks of three to four days so that you use up what you've got before you go shopping again. How well that works obviously depends how big your appetite is. If you eat up the leftovers your supplies won't last as long!

FRESHER'S MEAL PLANNER
(pp24-25)

This is a good simple plan to follow if you've just come up to uni. It will probably cost more than you'll spend normally but many ingredients will last several weeks.

VEGGIE MEAL PLANNER
(pp26-27)

A veggie shopping expedition can of course take exactly the same form as a non-veggie one but as a veggie you're probably rather more likely to use a wider variety of outlets and to buy fresh veg. You may well shop in health food stores or co-operatives (cheaper for nuts and pulses), street markets or even have a veg box. You may spot a bargain and build a number of meals around it just as a non-veggie would with meat. Vegetables can stretch just as effectively as a pack of mince.

That assumes of course, you know what to do with fresh veg when you buy them. If you're shopping for one it's worthwhile learning two or three things to do with veg that you can't buy in small quantities such as butternut squash or cauliflower so that you get maximum use out of them.

'5-A-DAY' HEALTHY EATING MEAL PLANNER (pp28-29)

Trying to build in at least 5 portions of fruit and veg a day makes it harder to stick to a budget so you need to be flexible. If you find that the fruit you want to use for a fruit salad is too expensive buy another kind instead. Or if pork is expensive that week, substitute chicken. Fresh produce also goes off more quickly so if you want to make it stretch take care to store it properly. Most veg are best stored in the fridge, exceptions being onion and garlic (the smell can taint other ingredients), potatoes (best stored in a cool, dark place) and tomatoes (better in a fruit bowl - they'll continue to ripen). And don't put bananas in the fridge. If you use half a fruit or vegetable, wrap the rest in Clingfilm and store for up to 48 hours (see more on storage on p30).

ELSEWHERE IN THE BOOK

There are lots of ideas for stretching dishes and recycling ingredients. See Everlasting Stew (p44), 1 Chicken = 6 Meals (p48), for example.

SHOPPING LIST

400–500g mince (enough for 3 meals)

2 x 400g tin of tomatoes (1 for the bolognese sauce plus a spare)

1 x pack spaghetti (enough for 4–5 meals)

1 x 500g pack basmati rice (enough for 6–10 meals)

200g tin of tuna (enough for 2 meals. Worth buying a multi pack if there's a good offer)

Frozen peas (a big – 900g – pack should last 2–4 weeks)

Sliced wholemeal loaf (should last most of the week)

200g cheddar (enough for 4–5 meals)

1 x 500g carton of natural yoghurt (will last all week; you can add fruit to make your own fruit yoghurts – see p78)

6 eggs (enough for 3–4 meals)

1 x 400g tin of kidney beans (enough for 2 meals)

A round lettuce or a small bag of salad (enough for 2 meals)

2–3 onions (you only need a couple but it's worth having one spare)

1/2 cucumber (or a whole one if it works out better value; lasts for several days)

2–3 tomatoes (buy loose, they're cheaper)

1 pepper (although may be better value to buy a bag)

3–4 bananas (for breakfasts, snacks and smoothies)

3–4 apples (for snacks and puds)

Mild chilli powder (should last all term)

A jar of clear honey (comparatively expensive but healthier than sugar and you can obviously use it as a spread)

Mild curry paste or powder (ditto)

Light soy sauce (a big bottle should last all term; buy in an Asian supermarket if you have one nearby)

A small to medium jar of mayo (depending which size is best value; will last a month once opened)

ASSUMING YOU HAVE THESE STORECUPBOARD BASICS

Garlic

Tomato paste

Some kind of dried herbs, preferably oregano/ Herbes de Provence

Sunflower oil

Wine vinegar

Salt and pepper

Butter or butter-type spread

Milk

Sugar

Lemon juice

OPTIONAL EXTRAS, DEPENDING ON FUNDS

Fresh oranges (buy a cheap plastic juicer and squeeze them by hand – much healthier than basic orange juice which is made from concentrate)

Fresh coriander (buy from an ethnic shop if you have one nearby – see p14)

DAY 1

Make a batch of Everlasting Mince (p42). Use a third of it to make Spaghetti Bolognese (p43), topping it with 25g (about a quarter of a small pack) of Cheddar cheese. Buy a simple round lettuce, take off the leaves you need for the salad, wash them and store the rest for a meal the next day. Make three times the **Budget Salad Dressing** on p61. Use one portion and keep the rest in a container or jam jar in the fridge for the next two days.

DAY 2

Turn one of the remaining portions of bolognese into a Chilli Con Carne (p43), using 1/2 a pepper and 1/2 the red kidney beans. Make another green salad with the rest of the lettuce and half the remaining salad dressing. For a packed lunch or snack you could make yourself a cheese and tomato sandwich using another 50g of the Cheddar and one of the tomatoes plus an apple.

DAY 3

Turn the final portion of bolognese into a Keema (see p43) and serve with rice (making enough for the following day). This would be good with an Onion Raita (scale down the recipe on p115). With the remaining kidney beans you could make a tuna and bean salad. Drain the tuna and mix half the contents of the tin with the remaining beans, a little chopped onion, tomato, the rest of the pepper and some chopped cucumber. Dress with the remaining salad dressing.

DAY 4

For your main meal make Egg-Fried Rice with the remaining rice (p86). For a packed lunch mix the remaining tuna with 1 tablespoons of mayo, 1 tablespoon of yoghurt and a little chopped onion. Use to make a wholemeal sandwich and top with sliced cucumber.

OTHER MEALS YOU COULD MAKE WITH WHAT YOU'VE BOUGHT

- **Spaghetti Napoli** (p36)
- **Egg mayo sandwich**
(p71 – using lettuce instead of cress)
- **Scrambled eggs** (p72)
- **Best ever cheese on toast** (p75)
- **Cheese and onion toastie** (p75)
- **Banana and honey sandwiches**
- **Banana smoothie**
Whizz a ripe banana up with 2 tablespoons of yoghurt, 1 teaspoon honey and the juice of 2 oranges.
- **Banana roughie**
(just squished banana, yoghurt and honey)
- **Pan-fried apple with honey and yoghurt**
Quarter and peel an apple, and cut into thick slices. Melt a little butter or butter spread in a small frying pan and fry for a minute or two. Stir in a teaspoon of sugar or honey and add a squeeze of lemon. Serve with yoghurt.

26 VEGGIE MEAL PLANNER

SHOPPING LIST

A pack of veggie burgers or felafel (enough for 2 meals)

A pack of wholemeal pitta bread (can be used instead of bread)

200g Cheddar or Lancashire cheese (enough for 4 meals)

A large carton of plain yoghurt (will last all week)

6 large eggs (for the frittata or other meals)

A cauliflower (2–3 meals)

2-3 potatoes (for the curry, with leftovers for the frittata)

$1/2$ a cucumber (or a whole one if better value)

2–3 fresh tomatoes (for the Arab salad and pitta pizzas)

A red pepper (for the Arab salad and frittata)

3 onions (for the dal, frittata and cauliflower curry)

A bunch of fresh coriander (See storage note on p115. Will really make all the difference to the way these meals taste. Remember, cheaper in an ethnic shop)

2-3 apples (for breakfasts and snacks)

500g red lentils (for the dal but also good for soup. Will make about 8 servings)

A pack of porridge oats (Should last at least a month, depending how often you make porridge)

A pack of dried raisins (for muesli or snacks)

Extra milk for the cauliflower cheese and porridge

Marigold vegetable bouillon powder (invaluable for stocks and stews. A tub lasts a couple of months)

A small bottle of lemon juice (useful to have to hand for salads and sharpening up sauces)

Ground cinnamon (always a good addition to apples but a pinch is good in tomato sauces too)

ASSUMING YOU HAVE THESE STORECUPBOARD BASICS

The storecupboard basics on p24, plus:

Curry paste or powder

Frozen peas

Mayonnaise

Plain flour

Soft brown sugar

OPTIONAL EXTRAS, DEPENDING ON FUNDS

Ground turmeric (good in vegetable curries and dals and as part of Moroccan spice mix – see p19)

Fresh ginger (good for curries and dals – will last a week in the fridge)

Fresh chillies (ditto)

Cumin seeds (add fragrance to curries and dals, particularly if dry-fried – i.e. warmed in a pan without any oil)

DAY 1

Divide the cauliflower into florets and boil or steam them until just tender (about 8 minutes). Use half for a Cauliflower Cheese (p63) and save the rest for making a curry the following day (see below).

DAY 2

Use the leftover cooked cauliflower to make a Cauliflower and Potato Curry (p63). Cook some extra potato for a Frittata the following day. With the curry you could serve Carrot Dal (p114) and toasted pitta bread (simply pop it in the toaster on a low setting). When the dal is cooked save a third for soup and a third to stuff another pitta bread for lunch the following day. Add some fresh coriander to the rest. For your other meal you could have veggie burgers or felafel with Arab Salad (p61). For a healthy breakfast try the Basic Muesli (p83) with some plain yoghurt

DAY 3

Use one portion of the remaining Carrot Dal to stuff a warmed, split pitta bread, adding slices of cucumber and a dollop of plain yoghurt. Your other meal could be a Frittata (open omelette) made with the leftover potato, onion, pepper and some frozen peas (see p72 – leave some to eat cold the next day). With another of the apples you could make a substantial breakfast of Apple and Cinnamon Porridge (p82).

DAY 4

A day for using up leftovers. Thin down the final portion of the Dal with some veggie stock to make soup. Serve with a swirl of yoghurt and chopped fresh coriander. For a snack you could cut up any leftover veggies like carrots, cucumber or peppers into crudités and serve them with a Garlic Mayo Dip (p61) Finish up the Frittata (a good breakfast). Or make a pitta 'pizza' – 1 or 2 wholemeal pitta breads, dry-fried in a frying pan to crisp and puff them up, topped with sliced tomato and grated cheddar and flashed under the grill.

OTHER MEALS YOU COULD MAKE WITH WHAT YOU'VE BOUGHT

• You could use the red lentils in a Winter Vegetable Soup (p46).
• If you have some leftover cauliflower cheese you could whizz it up with some vegetable stock to make a soup.
• Cheese and Onion Toasties or any of the other cheese recipes suggested on p75.
• Some of the egg-based meals suggested on pp72–73.

'5 A DAY' HEALTHY EATING SHOPPING LIST

2 (or 4 small) pork loin steaks (2 meals)

A pack of cooked ham (2–3 meals – will last 2–3 days after opening if wrapped well)

A 300g pack of frozen prawns (3–4 meals if kept in the freezer. The tiny North Atlantic prawns are the cheapest and just as tasty as those flashier king prawns)

A carton of low-fat fromage frais or large carton plain yoghurt (should last all week)

A medium carton of cottage cheese (for a salad and dip)

A pack of wholemeal rolls (substitute for bread)

3–4 carrots (for the stir-fry, salad, dip and soup)

A bunch of celery (lasts a week – enough for several meals including soup)

1–2 peppers (or a bag if it's better value – you can always roast them, see p64)

2–3 onions

A bunch of spring onions (for the stir-fry and pasta sauce)

3 ripe tomatoes or a 400g tin of tomatoes (2 meals)

2–3 Granny Smith apples

1/2 a melon or 2 pears

2 kiwi fruit and/or some green grapes

A small can of pineapple pieces in natural juice (2 meals)

A large can of apricot halves (2 meals)

Porridge oats (for Basic Muesli, see p83)

Raisins (see p83)

ASSUMING YOU HAVE THESE STORECUPBOARD BASICS

The storecupboard basics on p24, plus:

Light soy sauce
Tomato ketchup
Medium-hot curry paste
Vegetable bouillon powder
Spaghetti
Rice
Frozen peas

OPTIONAL EXTRAS, DEPENDING ON FUNDS

Fresh parsley (good to add to the soup, pilau and pasta sauce)

A pack of multigrain crispbread (optional addition to the rolls but useful to have around. If kept in a sealed tin it should last a couple of weeks)

DAY 1

Make **Sweet and Sour Pork**, following the recipe on p58, substituting pork for the chicken. Make enough rice to leave a portion to go with your meal the following night and make a pilau the following day. Make a **Green and White Fruit Salad** (p80). This should make enough for two meals.

DAY 2

Use the remaining pork to make South African-Style Pork with Apricots (p54), saving half the apricots for the following day. Microwave one portion of the leftover rice to accompany it and a portion of frozen peas. Eat the rest of the fruit salad. For your other meal you could have half a carton of cottage cheese with a crunchy salad made with grated carrot, and finely chopped spring onions, apple and celery (use the Dressing on p61, substituting lemon juice for the wine vinegar). Have a couple of multigrain crispbreads or a wholemeal roll with it. The leftover pineapple from the stir-fry would make a healthy breakfast with some fromage frais or yoghurt and a helping of Basic Muesli (p83) or other cereal.

DAY 3

Kick off the day with the leftover apricots from the pork with fromage frais or yoghurt and a helping of basic muesli or other cereal. For an easy lunch make a dip with the rest of the cottage cheese mixed with fromage frais or yoghurt and a little onion or crushed garlic. Cut up some fresh carrot, celery and pepper strips to dunk in it and serve with a wholemeal roll or crispbread. Use the final portion of leftover rice and a quarter of the frozen prawns to make Indian-style Quick-Spiced Rice (p86). Follow it with a kiwi fruit, some melon or a few grapes.

DAY 4

Use any leftover veggies like celery, onion and carrot to make a simple chunky soup, following the basic Winter Soup method on p46 but adding a handful of rice instead of beans. You should have enough left over for the following day. You could also have a wholemeal ham roll. For a main meal you could use another portion of the frozen prawns to make Spaghetti Marinara, using the recipe on p38, substituting prawns for the mixed seafood. It should make enough sauce to have some leftover for the following night with rice. Afterwards you could have a wedge of melon or other fruit. And continue the breakfast routine of some fresh fruit like grapes or apple with yoghurt or fromage frais and muesli.

OTHER MEALS YOU COULD MAKE WITH WHAT YOU'VE BOUGHT

• A plate of sliced ham and melon.
• Wholemeal rolls filled with cottage cheese and prawns.
• Prawn salad with peppers, celery, tomato and spring onions.
• Spaghetti Napoli (see p36)

You're only going to be able to make food stretch if you store and reheat it safely. Easier said than done I know. It's all too easy to fail to wrap food properly, or just leave it lying around instead of putting it away in the fridge.

It certainly helps to have the right kind of storage containers. A good basic selection would include: A range of small bowls and cups (easily obtainable from charity shops) and/or a set of different sized inexpensive plastic boxes (available from supermarkets). You'll also need a roll of Clingfilm, foil and some plastic bags (pick up a few of the free ones when you're next in the fruit and veg section of the supermarket).

MAKE SURE YOU:

 Get perishable food home as soon as possible after buying it.

 Quickly cool any cooked food you intend to store, then once it's completely cold, wrap it thoroughly so that it's airtight and put it in the fridge. NEVER put warm food in a fridge as it will raise the temperature of the other food in there. Also don't overload your fridge, as this will also affect the temperature. Fridges also need cleaning and defrosting occasionally!

 Bring any food you're reheating to boiling point then simmer for 2–3 minutes to make sure you kill off any bugs. (Or give it a good blast in the microwave).

 To be on the safe side eat up within the recommended periods below:

• **within 24 hours**
High risk foods such as shellfish and other fresh fish, raw mince, offal and pre-prepared salads, stir-fries and beansprouts that have reached their sell-by date
• **within 1–3 days**
chicken and other meat*, sausages (if wrapped), mushrooms, soft fruit such as strawberries, leftovers
• **within 4–6 days**
soft cheese, yoghurt, milk, tomatoes and other fresh veg
• **within 1 week – 10 days**
Bacon and ham (though consume within a couple of days once you open the pack) hard cheese, eggs
• **within 1 month or more**
Butter and spreads (check the use-by date)
Frozen foods (which should never be refrozen once thawed)

• **You can exceed these timings if you're ultra careful, as illustrated by the chicken recipes on pp48–53. But make the stock as soon as possible after you've used up the meat.**
• **REMEMBER: IF IN DOUBT CHUCK IT OUT!**

OTHER SAFETY TIPS

☠ Do wash your hands thoroughly with soap before starting to prepare food. Dry hands with a towel or kitchen towel rather than your tea towel.

☠ Do keep your working surfaces clean. Or use a clean chopping board if they're not. Give them a good blitz every couple of days with an anti-bacterial cleaner.

☠ Do keep the sink clean and free from teabags, potato peelings, leftover pasta and other grot.

☠ Do wash your tea towels regularly and replace the washing up brush and/or scourers before they get too squalid.

☠ Don't leave kitchen towel, tea towels or oven gloves near the hob where they can catch fire.

☠ Don't leave pan handles sticking out from the stove.

☠ Don't leave the hob, grill or appliances – such as sandwich toasters – on when you've finished cooking.

☠ Don't leave your toaster full of crumbs and your grill pan clogged with fat. It's asking for a flare-up.

☠ WHAT TO DO IF THE OIL IN A PAN CATCHES FIRE

Throw a damp towel over it to exclude the air. (Wring it out under the tap.) NEVER throw water on an oil fire. If it's out of control get everyone out of the kitchen, shut the door, leave the building and call 999.

32 OTHER USEFUL STUFF

People who have cooked a long time tend to take a great deal for granted, using terms that they perfectly understand but which may totally bewilder the person who's following the recipe. Here are a few:

 'BRING TO THE BOIL'
Usually used of liquid. Heat until bubbles break out over the surface.

 'SIMMER'
Used of things that have come to the boil. Cook over a low to moderate heat so that the liquid just trembles.

 'CHOP FINELY/ROUGHLY'
How small is fine? Well as small as you can get it basically. Roughly chopped means cutting into smallish pieces without any great precision

 'WHISK/BEAT'
Basically the action of getting air into the ingredients to increase the volume (usually done with a whisk) or amalgamating the different components in a mixture like a pancake batter or salad dressing together. (Can be done with a fork or a hand-held blender)

 'A DASH, A SHAKE'
Literally what comes out of a bottle if you give it a quick shake – a few drops, about $1/8$–$1/4$ of a teaspoon.

THE WAY THE RECIPES ARE WRITTEN

You'll see that many of the ingredients listed in the recipes are pre-prepared. That's partly to avoid repetition, partly to get over the idea that it helps to read through the recipe and get everything you need ready before you start cooking. So you may find to begin with that recipes take slightly longer than you anticipate. Once you've made a recipe once or twice though you'll find it much easier and quicker to prepare it. I've tried to explain each step in the recipe as clearly as possible without making them over-long but a lot of it is simple common sense. If you add a tin of whole tomatoes, for instance, and the desired result is a tomato sauce, then it makes sense to break the tomatoes down with a wooden spoon or a fork rather than leave them whole. Don't be intimidated by recipes though. They're just guidelines rather than rules. Feel free to adapt them.

MEASUREMENTS AND SYMBOLS

You don't need to use exact measurements but it can help if you're inexperienced. The easiest way is to acquire some scales, measuring spoons and a measuring jug but you can make do without:
• A teaspoon is the size of spoon you use for stirring tea or coffee or eating yoghurt out of a pot. A dessertspoon is the type you use to eat cereal or soup while a tablespoon is the size of spoon you would use for serving food. Put another way a teaspoon contains 5ml, a dessertspoon 10ml and a tablespoon 15ml.
• Spoons can be described in a recipe as 'level', 'rounded' or 'heaped'. 'Level' is where the contents of the spoon are literally level with the edge of the bowl of the spoon. 'Rounded' is where they are slightly domed and 'heaped' is where they're piled on the spoon. (You need to use a bit of common sense about this. You could for example get an absolutely massive tablespoon of, say, mashed potato which would be equivalent to about 3 or 4 ordinary tablespoons.) Some recipes also call for $1/2$ or $1/4$ teaspoons – usually for powerful ingredients like spices.
• A pinch is the amount you can hold between your thumb and forefinger and a handful is exactly that – the amount you can pick up and hold in your hand (without trying over-hard to cram it in).
• If you're doubling a recipe you don't always need to double the most powerful ingredients. If the original recipe calls for 1 teaspoon of curry paste you may not need as much as two. Try $1 1/2$ first. Same applies to salt and sugar. Always taste as you go.

Where you see this symbol ♥ the recipe is suitable for vegetarians. Where you see this symbol £ you'll find some great bit of budget advice, from how to stretch a meal to what to do with leftovers.

If there's anything you don't understand about one of the recipes don't hesitate to e-mail me at fiona@beyondbakedbeans.com.

SURVIVE

Even if you live in a shared house you probably do a fair amount of cooking just for yourself. It might be cheaper (it is!) to all pitch in, but sometimes you're all doing different things, or simply can't get organised enough to shop for a household. Many students (and non-students, come to that) also live by themselves so cooking for one is a lifestyle for many. Too often it becomes sheer drudgery – a joyless affair of heating up ready-meals, or living off the same food day after day. You don't buy fresh ingredients because you don't know what to do with them, or think you'll waste them.

It doesn't have to be like this. You can eat really well on a budget without spending all your time in the kitchen, or being a brilliant cook. Follow the easy meal planners (pp22-29), learn a few basic recipes, and how to give them a twist, and you'll both eat and feel better. Promise.

36 SPAGHETTI AND OTHER PASTA SHAPES

WHAT YOU CAN MAKE WITH A PACK OF SPAGHETTI

For some odd reason spaghetti is generally half the price of pasta shapes, maybe because it's trickier to eat and you can't turn it into a salad. A 500g pack provides at least five helpings (100g of spaghetti is enough for a hearty appetite – 75g will do if you're less hungry).

HOW TO COOK SPAGHETTI

Fill a large saucepan with boiling water from the kettle (quicker than boiling it in the pan). Add salt and then add the spaghetti pressing it down into the water as the ends soften until it is completely submerged. Stir it around with a large fork or spoon to keep the strands separated, continue to boil without stirring until it is cooked, following the instructions on the pack. Drain the spaghetti in a sieve or colander and, either tip it into the sauce, or pour the sauce over it, depending on the recipe.

SPAGHETTI NAPOLI (SIMPLE SPAGHETTI WITH TOMATO SAUCE)

Don't even think about buying a ready-made pasta sauce. These homemade versions are so much simpler and tastier. They both make more sauce than you'll need, but you can use the leftovers for other recipes.

WINTER VERSION ♥
Serves 1, + leftover sauce

2 tbsp vegetable oil, or olive oil if you have some
1 clove of garlic peeled and crushed
1 400g tin of whole tomatoes (usually cheaper than chopped tomatoes)
75–100g spaghetti
Salt and pepper to taste
Grated Parmesan or Cheddar to serve

Heat a large frying pan over a moderate heat, add the oil and heat through for a minute then add the crushed garlic and stir. Tip in the tomatoes and break them up with a fork or wooden spoon. Leave the sauce on a low heat while you cook the spaghetti, following the instructions on the pack. If the sauce seems a bit dry add a couple of spoonfuls of the pasta cooking water. Drain the spaghetti in a sieve or colander, tip onto a plate and pour over half the sauce. Sprinkle with grated cheese.

WHAT IS A CLOVE OF GARLIC?

The first big mistake I made when I was cooking! I thought a clove was the whole bulb or head. It isn't – it's one individual section of the bulb.

WHY NOT ADD...

• Stir in some fresh parsley at the end if you have some, or add half a teaspoon of dried oregano or Herbes de Provence when you add the garlic.

• Other good additions would be bacon, mushrooms, peppers or cubes of aubergine. Fry them at the beginning before you add the garlic.

£ LEFTOVER SAUCE?

Any leftover sauce can be used to top a piece of fried or grilled chicken or fish or to make a French bread pizza. Lightly toast both sides of a cut baguette, spread the tomato sauce over the cut side, top with grated cheese and grill.

SUMMER VERSION ✿
Serves 1, + leftover sauce

If you can get your hands on some really ripe tomatoes make your pasta sauce this way.

4 large ripe tomatoes (about 400g)
2 tbsp vegetable or olive oil
1 large clove of garlic, peeled and crushed
1 tbsp tomato paste
75–100g spaghetti
Salt and pepper
A few fresh basil leaves, shredded, if you can find some reduced (optional)

First, skin the tomatoes. Make a little cut in the skin near the stem, put them in a bowl and cover them with boiling water. After a minute, drain the tomatoes, pour cold water over them and peel off the skins. Chop them roughly. Heat a large frying pan over a moderate heat, add the oil, heat for a minute then add the crushed garlic and tomato paste.

Stir and then tip in the tomatoes, simmer over a low heat while you cook the spaghetti, following the instructions on the pack. If the sauce seems a bit dry, spoon in 3–4 tablespoons of the pasta cooking water. Drain the spaghetti in a sieve or colander, tip onto a plate and pour over half the sauce. Sprinkle over the basil, if using.

£ BULK IT OUT

• This type of sauce is often served without cheese but tastes good with crumbled goats' cheese.

• You could add some drained tinned tuna, or other seafood (see Spaghetti Marinara, overleaf).

SPAGHETTI MARINARA
Serves 1, + leftover sauce

Like the Summer Tomato Sauce (previous page), this authentic Italian seafood spaghetti is best made from July to September when tomatoes are really ripe. You should be able to find bags or packs of mixed seafood at a good price, but if you can't use cheap frozen prawns instead. The sauce makes enough for two helpings so save half for the following day to serve with rice.

3 tbsp vegetable or olive oil
1/2 a bunch of spring onions, trimmed and finely sliced, or a small onion, peeled and finely chopped
1 large clove of garlic, peeled and crushed
1 tbsp tomato paste
3 large ripe tomatoes (about 300g), skinned (see p37) and roughly chopped
75–100g spaghetti
200g mixed, frozen or thawed seafood, or seafood 'cocktail' containing e.g. prawns, mussels and squid
A handful of fresh parsley, or about 60g frozen peas
Salt and pepper
A few drops of wine vinegar to taste

Heat a large frying pan over a moderate heat, add the oil and fry the onion for a few minutes until soft. Add the crushed garlic and tomato paste, stir and tip in the tomatoes, simmer over a low heat while you cook the spaghetti, following the instructions on the pack.

If the sauce seems a bit dry add a couple of spoonfuls of the pasta cooking water. Using a fork, mash the tomatoes as they soften. About 5 minutes before the spaghetti is cooked, turn up the heat under the sauce and tip in the seafood and peas, if using. Stir and heat through thoroughly. Season and add the parsley, if using. Drain the spaghetti. Spoon off half the sauce for the following day's meal and tip the spaghetti into the remainder of the sauce. Toss together well and serve.

£ BARE STORECUPBOARD?

If you're desperate you can simply serve spaghetti with butter and grated cheese (preferably Parmesan), or with olive oil, garlic and chilli (the classic *spaghetti con olio e aglio*).

EXTRA CREAMY CARBONARA Serves 1

It really is worth investing in some fresh Parmesan (or the slightly cheaper Grana Padano) for this; it's a luxury, but it keeps well in the fridge and a little goes a long way. Cheddar doesn't quite hit the spot for this recipe.

1 tbsp cooking oil
4–5 streaky bacon rashers, or 2–3 back rashers, rinds removed and chopped (about 75g in total)
1 small to medium onion, peeled and finely chopped
2 eggs, preferably free-range
2 tbsp freshly grated Parmesan or Grana Padano plus extra for serving
75–100g dried spaghetti
2 tbsp double or whipping cream
Salt and ground black pepper

Heat the oil in a frying pan over a medium heat and fry the bacon until the fat begins to run. Add the onion, turn the heat down low and fry for another 5 minutes or until soft. Beat the eggs with 2 tablespoons of the Parmesan and season with pepper and a little salt. Cook the spaghetti in plenty of boiling water following the instructions on the pack. Once it's cooked, drain it thoroughly, saving a bit of the cooking water and return it to the pan off the heat. Quickly tip in the bacon, onion and beaten eggs and mix thoroughly so the egg 'cooks' in the hot pasta. Add the cream and a spoonful or two of the cooking water, add extra seasoning if needed then serve immediately with extra Parmesan.

WHY NOT ADD...
• A few frozen peas. Pop them in once you've cooked the onion.

WHY NOT SWITCH...
• The bacon for chopped, cooked ham – just add it to the onions to heat through.
• For a veggie version, fry 3–4 sliced or chopped mushrooms in place of the bacon.

£ WHAT TO DO WITH THE REST OF THE CREAM
• Stir a spoonful into your porridge.
• Use to top stewed fruit like apples or plums (see p78).
• Work some into a mashed banana and sprinkle with brown sugar.
• Stir some into a savoury sauce (see p100), adding a squeeze of lemon if you want the effect of crème fraîche or soured cream.
• Make a wicked toffee sauce (see p134).

USING PASTA SHAPES

The advantage of using pasta shapes is that you can simply adapt the dish you've made into a pasta salad for the following day.

PASTA TWISTS WITH TUNA, LEMON AND PARSLEY
Serves 1 + leftovers

This is a dish to make when you've got a bottle of olive oil in the cupboard; it needs decent oil.

150–200g pasta twists or bows (farfalle)
Half a bunch (4–5) spring onions or 1 leek
2–3 tbsp olive oil
185g tin of tuna, drained
Grated rind and juice of half a lemon, preferably unwaxed
A handful of fresh parsley or coriander (about 20g), finely chopped
Salt and pepper to serve

Bring a kettle of water to the boil, pour into a saucepan and bring back to boiling point. Add a little salt, add the pasta, stir and cook for the time recommended on the pack. Trim the ends and tops off the spring onions and cut them in half, or quarter them lengthways, depending on how thick they are. Cut across into 4 or 5 pieces to give fine, short shreds. (Or, if using a leek, trim, finely slice and wash.) Heat 2 tablespoons of the olive oil in a small pan, add the onion and cook gently for a minute or two until softened. Add the drained tuna, lemon rind and parsley, stir and leave over a low heat. When the pasta is cooked, spoon 3–4 tablespoons of the pasta cooking water into the sauce and drain the rest. Return the pasta to the saucepan, tip in the tuna sauce and toss well together. Serve half the pasta, adding a little extra olive oil, pepper and possibly salt to taste (though the tuna may be quite salty). Cool the remainder, cover with cling film and refrigerate.

£ LEFTOVER SALAD
PASTA SALAD WITH TUNA, LEMON AND PARSLEY

Ideally, bring the pasta to room temperature about an hour before you want to eat. You can eat it just as it is, or stir in a tablespoon of mayo, mixed with a tablespoon of plain yoghurt.

HOT PENNE WITH RED PEPPERS AND 'FAKE FETA' 🌱
Serves 1 + leftovers

Easy to vary this recipe depending on what you have to hand. Obviously you need peppers but otherwise anything with a bit of a kick will work. The 'Fake Feta'? Caerphilly marinated in salt and lemon juice (see below); same effect for half the price.

3 tbsp of oil including some of the oil from the sun-dried tomatoes, if using

1 medium onion (about 125–150g), peeled and roughly chopped

1 large or 2 smaller red peppers, quartered, de-seeded and roughly chopped

150–200g penne or other pasta shapes (wholewheat pasta is nice with this recipe)

1 large clove of garlic, peeled and crushed

1/2 tsp hot paprika or a dash of chilli sauce

1/2 a large tin of chopped or whole tomatoes

4 sun-dried tomatoes in oil, halved, drained and finely chopped and/or 10–12 pitted black olives, roughly chopped (both optional but good)

50g 'Fake Feta' cheese (Caerphilly or Wensleydale see opposite)

1–2 tbsp chopped fresh parsley (optional)

Salt and pepper

Heat a large frying pan or wok, add the oil and tip in the chopped onion and peppers. Fry over a moderate heat for about 7–8 minutes until both the vegetables are beginning to char at the edges. Meanwhile, put the pasta on to cook for the time recommended on the packet (usually about 10 minutes). Once the peppers and onion are cooked, add the crushed garlic and paprika or chilli sauce. Stir, then add the tinned tomatoes (breaking them down with a fork if whole), sun-dried tomatoes and olives, if using. Bring back to a simmer and cook for about 5 minutes while the pasta finishes cooking, adding 3–4 tablespoons of the pasta cooking water if the sauce seems too dry. Stir in the parsley, if using, and season with salt and pepper. Drain the pasta, reserving a little more of the water. Return the pasta to the saucepan, tip in the sauce, and toss well together.

Transfer half the pasta into a bowl, stir in a little of the reserved pasta water to moisten. Allow it to cool and then refrigerate. Spoon the remaining pasta onto a large plate, crumble over the 'Fake Feta' and serve.

£ FAKE FETA

Crumbly white English cheeses such as Caerphilly and Wensleydale can be made to taste like the more expensive Feta. Just cut into cubes, sprinkle with salt, and squeeze over a little lemon, mix lightly and leave for 10–15 minutes. You can also substitute it for Feta in a Greek salad or in a mixed bean salad.

£ LEFTOVER SALAD
PASTA SALAD WITH RED PEPPERS AND 'FAKE FETA'

Take the remaining portion of pasta, add a little extra parsley and another 50g of 'Fake Feta'. Mix together and serve at room temperature.

A basic batch of mince can be made to stretch for 3–4 meals. And with a little bit of tweaking it'll taste different every time.

BUYING MINCE

Pack sizes vary for mince so use whichever is the best deal, whether it's 400g, 450g or 500g. 400g will make 3 meals, 500g might make 4 if you refrigerate it carefully.

BASIC BOLOGNESE
Makes 3–4 meals for 1

A simple Bolognese sauce you can serve with spaghetti or other pasta or as a baked potato topping.

1 tbsp oil
400–500g beef mince
1 heaped tbsp concentrated tomato puree
1–2 cloves of garlic, peeled, crushed or finely chopped
1 level tsp oregano or Herbes de Provence
1 400g tin of tomatoes
Salt and pepper

Heat a frying pan over a moderately high heat for 2–3 minutes. Add the oil, swirl round the pan then add half the mince spreading it around. Fry until beginning to brown then turn it over with a wooden spoon or spatula. Keep frying until all the mince is browned (about 1½–2 minutes). Tipping the pan away from you so the fat runs away, scoop out the mince onto a large plate.

Pour the fat that has accumulated in the pan into a cup or bowl to discard later. Put the pan back on the hob and repeat with the remaining mince, discarding the fat again at the end. Turn down the heat a little and return all the meat to the pan without any further oil. Add the tomato paste and stir into the meat until it is well distributed, stirring it all the time. Add the garlic, herbs and the tinned tomatoes, breaking them up with a fork. Season with salt and pepper, bring to a simmer then turn the heat right down and leave to cook gently for about 15 minutes. Spoon out a quarter to a third of the sauce to make spaghetti Bolognese (see over) then divide the remaining sauce into 2 or 3 portions, cool and refrigerate them (ready to be used for Meals 2, 3 and 4, see opposite).

MEAL 1
WITH SPAGHETTI OR PASTA

You need 75–100g dried spaghetti or pasta shapes and some grated cheese. Cook the spaghetti as described on p36. Top with a quarter to a third of the Bolognese and sprinkle with grated cheese – Parmesan if you have some, otherwise Cheddar. See also Budget Bolognese (pp94–95.

MEAL 2
A MINI SHEPHERDS PIE

You need a medium to large potato and some Marmite. Cut a medium to large potato into 6–8 pieces, cover with cold water and bring to the boil. Cook for about 12–15 minutes until you can easily insert a knife through the potato pieces. Drain the potato, cut it up roughly and mash with a fork. Add a little warm milk and butter and season with salt and pepper.

Meanwhile take a quarter to a third of the Bolognese mixture and put it in a small saucepan. Stir in half a teaspoon of Marmite (no more – it'll be too salty) dissolved in a tablespoon of hot water. Bring to the boil and simmer for 5 minutes. Heat up the grill. Put the mince in a small heatproof bowl or dish and cover with the mash. Pop the pie under the grill and brown. Serve.

MEAL 3
CHILLI CON CARNE

You need half a pepper, a tin of red kidney beans and some mild chilli powder. Cut the pepper into small pieces. Heat a small frying pan, add a little oil (about 1 tablespoon) and fry the pepper for 3–4 minutes until beginning to soften. Add a teaspoon of mild chilli powder and $1/4$ teaspoon of ground cumin, if you have some, and stir. Mix in a quarter to a third of the Basic Bolognese. Drain a 400g tin of red kidney beans and rinse the beans under cold running water. Add half the beans to the mince. (Save the remainder for a salad – see p25.) Add 2 tablespoons of water, stir, and heat through until boiling. Turn the heat down and simmer for 5 minutes. Serve on it's own or with boiled rice (see p86).

MEAL 4
KEEMA (SPICY MINCE WITH PEAS)

You need some curry paste or powder and frozen peas. Fresh coriander is a good addition if you have some. Take a quarter to a third of the Bolognese mixture and put it in a small saucepan. Add half a mug of frozen peas, $1/2$–1 teaspoon of curry paste or powder and 2 tablespoons of water and heat through until boiling. Turn the heat down, simmer for 5 minutes, then stir in some fresh coriander if you have some. Serve with rice or naan and an onion or cucumber raita (see p115).

Everlasting stew... well, not quite everlasting, but you could eke this out for 3 days, which isn't bad for a recipe based on a very small amount of meat and a few root veg. It takes a long time to cook – cheap meat can be tough – but you can go off and leave it bubbling away. Be sure to use fresh rather than frozen veg – frozen will disintegrate over the long cooking time.

BASIC STEW
Makes up to 3 meals for 1

300–350g braising steak
3 tbsp oil
2 medium-sized onions, peeled and roughly chopped
1/2 tsp dried thyme
1 level tbsp plain flour
1 1/2 level tsp Marmite
2 medium-sized carrots, peeled and sliced
A few turnips, a parsnip or 1/2 a medium-sized swede (about 250g), peeled and cut into cubes
Salt, ground black pepper
A few drops of wine vinegar

Cut any excess fat off the braising steak and cut into small cubes. Heat a heavy casserole or lidded frying pan and add 2 tablespoons of the oil. Tip in the meat and fry quickly on all sides. Remove the meat from the pan with a large spoon. Pour the fat into a cup and discard later. Set aside the meat. Add a little extra oil, turn the heat down and add the onions to the pan. Cook them for 2 or 3 minutes then stir in the thyme and flour. Stir the Marmite into 350ml of boiling water until it has dissolved, then add this stock to the onion and bring to the boil. Add the sliced carrots and cubed turnips, parsnip or swede and return to the pan. Add the meat to the pan and bring back to the boil. Turn the heat right down and cover the pan. Leave to cook, barely bubbling over a low heat for 3–4 hours until the meat and vegetables are tender, stirring the stew occasionally. Check seasoning adding salt, pepper and a few drops of vinegar to taste. Served with boiled or mashed potatoes.

DAY 2
ADD SOMETHING TOMATOEY

Enliven your leftovers with a tablespoon of tomato paste diluted in half a cup of hot water or 2–3 chopped tinned tomatoes or even a couple of tablespoons of ketchup. Add some crushed garlic and ½ a tin of cannellini or borlotti beans (make a bean salad with the remaining beans). Add extra water if it seems too thick and reheat slowly. Simmer for 10 minutes then serve.

DAY 3
ADD SOMETHING SPICY

Try a teaspoon of curry paste or curry powder, half a mug of frozen peas and a squeeze of lemon. Simmer for 10 minutes and serve with rice (make twice as much rice as you need and make egg-fried rice with the rest – see p86).

£ PACK IT IN
Sometimes a stew pack, if reduced, will be cheaper than buying the vegetables individually.

WHAT ELSE CAN YOU DO WITH ROOT VEG?
• Roast 'em. Just peel and cut them up into even-sized pieces and roast for about 50 minutes to an hour. Carrots, onions, parsnips and potatoes are particularly good together.
• Mash 'em. Peel and cut them into cubes, boil till tender (15–20 minutes depending on the veg), drain and mash, or whizz in a food processor (except for spuds – it makes them gluey). Swede and carrot are good together. Mashed parsnips are great with cream.
• Grill 'em – parsnips are fab, half boiled, then trickled with honey and grilled.
• Make soup from them (see Simple Seasonal Soups, p46).

46 SIMPLE SEASONAL SOUPS

If you can cut up vegetables you can make soup. The trick is tailoring what you buy to the time of year. That way you get the best value and maximum flavour.

WINTER SOUP ✿
Serves 1–2

Veg that work well in winter soups are onions, carrots, swedes, celery, leeks, potatoes and dark leafy greens.

3 tbsp sunflower or vegetable oil
1 onion, peeled and roughly chopped or 1 leek, trimmed sliced and well washed
1 carrot, peeled and thinly sliced
1–2 sticks of celery, trimmed and sliced (optional)
1/4 swede or 1 medium-sized potato, peeled and cut into small cubes
500ml of hot vegetable stock made with 1 level tbsp vegetable bouillon powder or – if you're not veggie – 500ml homemade Chicken Stock (see p52)
1/2 a 400g tin cannelini, haricot or butter beans, drained, rinsed
Salt and ground black pepper
3 tbsp chopped fresh parsley or a handful of finely sliced greens

Heat the oil over a moderate heat in a large saucepan, add the chopped vegetables, stir well, turn the heat down to low, cover the pan and cook for 10–15 minutes. Pour in the hot stock, bring to the boil and simmer for another 15–20 minutes until the vegetables are well cooked, adding the beans, if using, for the final 5 minutes. Season with salt and pepper and stir in some parsley or finely sliced greens. Simmer for another 2 minutes and serve.

TRY THIS TOO...
Add 2 rashers chopped bacon to the oil and cook for a couple of minutes before you fry the veg.

£ LEFTOVERS
Spice up any leftovers with 1 tsp Moroccan Spice Mix (p19) or 1/4 tsp curry paste or curry powder. Add 200ml of passata or 1/2 a 400g tin of whole tomatoes, crushed or chopped.

SPRING SOUP ✿
Serves 1–2

Fresh tasting, creamy and buttery, this is really simple to make with a mixture of fresh and frozen veg. Use up any broccoli or cauliflower stalks or the lower end of asparagus stalks which otherwise tend to get wasted.

1 tbsp sunflower or other light cooking oil
A good slice (about 25g) butter
1/2 bunch of spring onions or 1 leek, trimmed, sliced and well washed
A few broccoli, cauliflower and/or asparagus stalks, peeled and sliced (optional)
100g fresh or frozen broad beans
75g of frozen peas
450ml hot vegetable stock made with 2 tsp vegetable bouillon powder or – if you're not veggie – 450ml homemade Chicken Stock (p52)
A few shredded spinach leaves or 2 tbsp finely chopped parsley
Salt, pepper and lemon juice
A little double cream (optional)

Heat the oil gently in a large saucepan then add the butter, tip in the vegetables, stir well, cover and cook for 5 minutes. Pour in the hot stock bring to the boil and simmer for about 8–10 minutes or until the veg are tender but still bright green, adding the spinach leaves or parsley about 3 minutes before the end of the cooking time. Season to taste with salt, pepper and lemon juice, stirring in a little cream if you have some.

£ LEFTOVERS

You could add some cooked rice to the leftovers to make this more substantial.

SUMMER SOUP ✿
Serves 1–2

Use Mediterranean vegetables like tomatoes, peppers and courgettes to give this soup more of an Italian feel.

3 tbsp olive oil or other cooking oil
1 onion, peeled and roughly chopped
1 red pepper, de-seeded and chopped or $1/2$ a red pepper and $1/2$ a green pepper
1 large clove of garlic, peeled and crushed or finely chopped
$1/2$ tsp dried oregano or Herbes de Provence if not using fresh herbs
2–3 fresh ripe tomatoes, skinned and chopped (see p37) or $1/2$ a 400g tin of plum tomatoes or 200ml of passata (in which case use less stock)
1 medium-sized courgette, trimmed and sliced
75g fresh or frozen sweetcorn kernels (optional)
450ml hot vegetable stock made with 2 tsp vegetable bouillon powder or – if you're not veggie – 450ml homemade Chicken Stock (p52)
Salt and pepper
Some fresh basil (if available cheaply) or 2 tbsp chopped parsley
Grated Parmesan, Grana Padano or Cheddar to serve

Heat the oil over a moderate heat in a large saucepan, add the chopped onion and pepper and stir. Turn the heat down to low, cover the pan and cook for 5–6 minutes, until the vegetables are starting to soften. Add the garlic and oregano if you don't have any fresh herbs and cook for a minute then add the tomatoes, the sliced courgettes, sweetcorn, if using, and stock. Bring to the boil and simmer for another 10–15 minutes until the vegetables are cooked. Season to taste with salt and pepper and add a few shredded basil leaves, or a couple of tablespoons of parsley, if you have some. Simmer for another 2 minutes then serve with grated Parmesan, Grana Padano or Cheddar.

£ LEFTOVERS

Add some lightly cooked green beans, cooked pasta or $1/2$ a tin of drained, rinsed cannellini beans to any leftovers.

You might not believe it but it is actually possible to make at least six meals for 1 from a chicken. Not convinced? Well, first of all it helps to know a bit about the bird's anatomy. The prime bits of a chicken are the two breasts, either side of the backbone. They're the most lean and tender bits.

You can eat one hot when you roast it – see p90 – (Meal 1) and the other one cold the following day, either as part of a salad (Meal 2) or in sandwiches.

Then there are the two legs. The fatter bit nearer the body is the thigh and contains lean, but slightly darker meat, that lends itself well to reheating in a curry or a pasta bake (Meal 3). The lower part of the leg is the drumstick, which, like the two wings, has slightly tougher, darker but still very tasty meat that can be used in a pilaf (Meal 4) or other rice dish. The carcass will still have some meat on it. You can make enough stock with that to make a soup (Meal 5) and a noodle dish (you guessed it – Meal 6).

A WORD OF WARNING!
Obviously to eke it out this far you need to be scrupulously careful about the way you store your chicken, cooling it down as quickly as possibly, wrapping it carefully, storing it in a fridge that's running at the right temperature and reheating it thoroughly. But if you do, it's one of the most economical ways to eat.

BREASTS

MEAL 1
LEMON ROAST CHICKEN BREAST WITH SAUTEED POTATOES

Roast a chicken, following the recipes on p90. Cut off one of the breasts for your first meal and serve with sautéed potatoes.

1 medium-large potato (about 250–300g)
Vegetable or other light cooking oil
Salt
1 cooked chicken breast (see p90)

SAUTEED POTATOES
Serves 1

Peel and cut the potatoes into thin slices about the depth of a 10p coin. Tip them into a bowl of cold water, swirl them around then drain them and dry them in a clean tea towel. Meanwhile, pour enough oil into a wok to give you a depth of about 2.5 cm, heat for about 2–3 minutes until hot enough to fry a piece of bread in about 30 seconds. Tip the potato slices into the oil and fry, turning them regularly until nicely browned – about 4–5 minutes. Spoon them out of the wok and onto some paper kitchen towel for a few seconds, to soak up any excess oil. Sprinkle with salt and serve with your Lemon Roast Chicken breast.

TRY THIS TOO...
Finely sliced parsnips and sweet potatoes taste great this way too.

MEAL 2 (OPTION 1)
SPICY CHICKEN SALAD (AKA CORONATION CHICKEN)

Invented, apparently, to celebrate the Queen's coronation in 1953. Call it Republican Chicken if you prefer.

1 cooked chicken breast
(skin removed, cut into strips)
1/4 of a cucumber, peeled, deseeded and cut into strips
1/2 a carrot, peeled and cut into fine strips
2 spring onions, trimmed, quartered and cut across into short pieces
Crisp lettuce leaves
A few chopped cashew nuts or unsalted roasted peanuts (optional)

For the dressing
1/4–1/2 tsp mild to medium hot curry paste or powder
1/2 tsp tomato ketchup
1 heaped tbsp mayonnaise
1 heaped tbsp plain yoghurt
1 heaped tbsp apricot jam
A little salt

First mix the ingredients for the dressing thoroughly together in a bowl, adding a teaspoon of water. Pour over the prepared chicken and vegetables and toss together. Lay a few crisp iceberg or Little Gem lettuce leaves on a plate and spoon over the salad. Sprinkle over a few chopped nuts if you have some.

MEAL 2 (OPTION 2)
BANG BANG CHICKEN

Basically the same basic ingredients as for Spicy Chicken Salad, but with an even punchier dressing.

1 cooked chicken breast and vegetables list from Spicy Chicken Salad
2 tbsp crunchy peanut butter
3–4 tbsp vegetable stock made with 1/4 tsp vegetable bouillon powder
1 tbsp fresh lime or lemon juice
1/2–1 tsp soy sauce
1 small clove of garlic, peeled and crushed
1–2 tsp sweet chilli sauce or a few drops of hot pepper sauce

Put the peanut butter in a bowl and work in 2–3 tablespoons of vegetable stock until you have a smooth sauce. Add the lime or lemon juice, soy sauce and crushed garlic and beat again. Season to taste with sweet chilli sauce or a few drops of hot pepper sauce. Mix with the chicken and prepared vegetables.

LEGS

MEAL 3
CHICKEN AND LEEK
PASTA BAKE Serves 1–2

Basically a macaroni cheese with chicken and leeks.

75g dried pasta quills or other shapes
25g butter
1 medium leek (about 175g), trimmed, finely sliced and well rinsed
1 tbsp flour
175ml semi-skimmed milk
1 cooked chicken thigh
50g mature Cheddar
Salt and ground black pepper

Bring a pan of water to the boil, add salt and tip in the pasta, stir and boil for the time recommended on the pack. While the pasta is cooking, melt the butter in another pan, add the sliced leeks and cook for a couple of minutes until soft. Stir in the flour, cook for a minute then stir in the milk. Bring to the boil then turn the heat down and simmer for 3–4 minutes until the sauce thickens. Remove any chicken skin from the thigh and strip the meat off the bone (saving the bone for stock – see p52). Cut the meat into small pieces, add to the sauce and heat through for about 3 minutes so that the chicken is thoroughly cooked.

Turn on the grill. Drain the pasta. Take the sauce off the heat and stir in the pasta and half the cheese. Season with salt and pepper and then tip into an ovenproof dish. Sprinkle over the remaining cheese and flash under the grill until the top is nicely browned and bubbling.

WHY NOT ADD...
Some chopped ham or crispy fried bacon to the sauce.

MEAL 4
CHICKEN AND MUSHROOM PILAU
Serves 1

Pilaus or pilafs make an excellent receptacle for the last bits of meat on a chicken – the drumsticks and wings.

3 tbsp vegetable or sunflower oil

1 small onion or $1/2$ a medium onion, peeled and finely chopped

$1/2$ tsp curry paste or powder

75g basmati rice

1–2 cooked chicken drumsticks or

1 cooked chicken thigh

1 clove of garlic, peeled and crushed (optional)

5–6 button mushrooms, rinsed and chopped

50g frozen peas

Salt and lemon juice to taste

Heat 1 tablespoon of the oil and cook the onion over a medium heat for about 6–7 minutes, stirring occasionally until it starts to brown. Stir in the curry paste and cook for another minute. Add the rice, stir and cook for a few seconds then pour in 150ml boiling water. Stir once, cover the pan tightly with a lid or a piece of foil, turn the heat down and cook for about 15 minutes until the water has been absorbed. Meanwhile, remove any skin off the chicken, strip the meat off the bones (saving them for stock – see p52) and cut it into small pieces. Heat the remaining oil in a small frying pan, add the crushed garlic, if using, stir and then add the chopped chicken and mushrooms. Stir-fry for 2–3 minutes, then add the peas and continue to cook over a low heat, adding a couple of tablespoons of water if the mixture gets too dry.

When the rice is cooked, mix the chicken, mushroom and pea mixture into the rice, replace the lid and leave off the heat for 5 minutes. Check the seasoning, adding a squeeze of lemon juice and salt to taste. If you have any fresh coriander, chop some and fork that through too.

TRY THESE TOO...

PRAWN AND MUSHROOM PILAU

Substitute frozen prawns for the chicken.

VEGGIE PILAU 🍃

You can make a veggie pilau in a similar way. Just leave out the chicken (obviously) and add some chopped dried apricots, raisins or a few chopped cashew nuts.

OR MAKE A STIR-FRY...
See p58.

BODY

CHICKEN STOCK

Given the well documented, health benefits of chicken soup it seems crazy to chuck away the carcass from your bird which can be made into a tasty stock. Admittedly, the cooking smells can be offputting so make sure the pan is half-covered which will also prevent the stock from boiling too fast. Ideally, stock is best made the day before you intend to use it so you can skim off any fat. Save the bones from any chicken joints you've stripped the meat off and chuck them in as well.

1 cooked chicken carcass
1 onion, peeled and quartered
1 carrot, peeled and cut into
  3 or 4 pieces
A few peppercorns or a bay leaf
  if you have them

Remove any herbs or lemon you might have tucked into the carcass when roasting it, and put it in a saucepan with the quartered onion and carrot. Pour in just enough cold water to cover the bones and bring slowly to the boil. As it nears boiling point you'll find froth forms on the surface – just skim it off with a spoon. Once the stock is at boiling point add the peppercorns and bay leaf, if using, partially cover the pan and leave over a low heat so the stock is still cooking but not boiling fast (it should barely tremble). Cook for about an hour to an hour and a half, checking it occasionally to make sure it's not cooking too slowly, or too fast. Strain the stock into a bowl and leave to cool. Ideally, refrigerate it at this point which makes it easier to remove any fat which has accumulated, otherwise, run a large spoon over the surface of the stock several times to remove the clear layer of fat which will have risen to the top of the bowl. The stock is now ready to use in all sorts of soups and in any dish where a chicken stock is required. It will keep for about 24 hours in the fridge or you can freeze it. (Place in an ice cube tray and you can take out exactly the amount of stock you need.)

TRY THIS TOO...

Soup made from fresh chicken bones. Ask a butcher for some carcasses and a few chicken wings (or buy a pack of wings). Roast them in a hot oven until browned then transfer to a saucepan and cover with cold water as described above.

MEAL 5
CLASSIC CHICKEN SOUP
Serves 1–2

1 tbsp oil
1 tbsp butter (about 15g)
1 medium onion peeled and
  sliced, or 1 leek, trimmed and
  sliced
1–2 carrots, peeled and cut into
  thin slices
350ml homemade Chicken
  Stock (see above)
A little cooked chicken meat
  (optional)
1–2 tsp vegetable bouillon
  powder if needed
Salt, pepper and lemon to taste
1–2 tbsp finely chopped parsley
  (optional but nice)

Heat the oil in a saucepan and add the butter, then once it has melted stir in the chopped vegetables. Stir well, turn the heat down to low and cover the pan. Cook for about 8–10 minutes. Pour in the chicken stock, bring to the boil then lower the heat and simmer for another 15–20 minutes until the vegetables are well cooked, adding the chicken, if using, about 5 minutes before the end of the cooking time. Check the seasoning. If the chicken taste is a bit weak, take a couple of tablespoons of the liquid and mix it with a teaspoon or two of vegetable bouillon powder and return the liquid to the pan. Season the soup with salt, pepper and a small squeeze of lemon and stir in the parsley, if using.

£ BULK IT OUT

You could add a small handful of rice, small pasta shapes or broken-up spaghetti when you add the stock.

SEE ALSO...
Simple Seasonal Soups, pp46-47.

MEAL 6
SPICY CHICKEN NOODLE SOUP
Serves 1–2

You can also jazz chicken stock up into a really tasty Asian-style noodle dish.

350ml chicken stock
1 clove of garlic, finely sliced
A small chunk of fresh ginger, peeled and finely sliced
A fresh chilli, de-seeded and finely sliced
A few crushed coriander stalks and/or a couple of roots, well washed and roughly chopped
A little cooked chicken meat or a few frozen prawns (optional)
Some finely sliced pak choi or cabbage or half a small pack of stir-fry veg
1–2 tsp light soy sauce or nam pla (Thai fish sauce)
Lemon or lime juice to taste (lime juice is better if using fish sauce) plus hot pepper sauce if you haven't used a chilli
50g rice noodles, cooked following the instructions on the pack
Fresh coriander leaves

Put the chicken stock in a saucepan and add the garlic, ginger, chilli and coriander stalks, if using. Bring to the boil, reduce the heat to very low and leave for 20–30 minutes. Strain the stock then return it to the saucepan with the chicken meat or prawns, greens or stir-fry veg. Bring back to the boil and simmer for 2 minutes. Season to taste with the soy sauce or nam pla, lemon or lime juice and hot chilli sauce. Put the cooked noodles in a large deep bowl (or half the noodles in a smaller bowl) and pour over the hot stock. Sprinkle over some fresh coriander leaves.

NO NOODLES?
You can use cooked spaghetti instead (see p36).

Pork chops are one of the best meat bargains around which you can cook in any number of ways. Especially tasty with some kind of fruit, or veg of course....

FRENCH-STYLE PORK CHOPS WITH CREAM AND MUSTARD Serves 1

A classic bistro-style dish.

1 tbsp vegetable, sunflower or olive oil
1 tbsp soft butter (about 15g)
1 pork chop or 2 small pork loin steaks
125g chestnut or button mushrooms, rinsed and sliced
100ml vegetable stock, made with 1/2 tsp vegetable bouillon
1/4 tsp dried thyme (optional)
1 tsp Dijon mustard
2 tbsp double cream
Ground black pepper and lemon juice

Heat a medium-sized frying pan and add the oil. When it's hot add the butter, then lay the pork chop in the pan. Brown for about 3 minutes on each side, then turn the heat down and cook for a further 2–3 minutes on each side, depending on how thick the chop is. Remove from the pan and set aside on a plate. Cook the mushrooms in the remaining oil and butter until lightly browned. Scoop them out and add to the pork. Pour in the stock, add the thyme and bubble up until the liquid has reduced by about two thirds. Take the pan off the heat and stir in the mustard and cream, then warm through gently, taking care not to let the sauce boil. Return the chop and the mushrooms to the pan together with any juices. Season with black pepper and add a little lemon juice. Heat through for another couple of minutes and then serve. Good with boiled potatoes and green beans.

£ SPARE MUSHROOMS?
See p62.

SOUTH AFRICAN-STYLE PORK CHOPS WITH APRICOTS Serves 1–2

South Africans are big on fruit and meat, particularly if it has a spicy twist. This is like a Cape Malay curry – mild and fruity.

1–2 tbsp vegetable or sunflower oil
1–2 pork chops or pork loin steaks
1 small onion, peeled and roughly chopped
1 stick of celery, trimmed and finely sliced or half a red pepper, de-seeded and finely sliced
1 tsp medium-hot curry paste
1 tbsp tomato ketchup
A small tin of apricots or 1/2 a 400g tin, drained and sliced
100ml chicken or vegetable stock made with 1/2 tsp vegetable bouillon powder

Heat a medium-sized frying pan and add the oil. When it's hot lay the pork chop in the pan. Brown for about 3 minutes on each side, then turn the heat down and cook for a further 2–3 minutes on each side depending how thick it is. Remove from the pan and set aside on a plate. Tip in the chopped onion and celery or pepper, adding a little bit more oil if needed. Fry over a moderate heat for about 5 minutes until they start to soften. Stir in the curry paste and tomato ketchup, add the sliced apricots then pour in the stock. Bring to the boil and simmer for 5 minutes then return the chop(s) to the pan and heat through. Serve with rice.

WEST COUNTRY-STYLE PORK CHOPS

A similar idea to the South African – style pork chops (see opposite) just leave out the curry paste and tomato ketchup and substitute a peeled, sliced apple for the apricots. If you have some cider around use it to replace half the stock. You could also stir a spoonful of cream in at the end.

SWEET AND SOUR PORK CHOPS

Cook the chops as opposite then use the stir-fry sauce on p58 (minus the chicken, obviously). If you are using pork loin steaks you could cut them into strips, instead of leaving them whole (removing any fat first).

Fresh fish is expensive but a pack of frozen fish fillets or steaks can make a number of meals with the added advantage of neither bones or skin to contend with. Even if you're not already a fish fan, give it a try.

7 WAYS TO COOK A FISH FILLET OR FISH STEAK

• Heat a tablespoon of oil and a slice of butter and fry it on both sides. Add a good squeeze of lemon and some chopped parsley. Serve with new potatoes and/or a salad.

• Spoon over 2–3 tablespoons of either of the tomato sauces on pp36-37 and some black olives if you have some and microwave it, or, heat it through in a pan as above. Good with rice.

• Add half the 'Summer' tomato sauce (pp36-37) and $1^1/_2$ teaspoons of Moroccan Spice Mix (p19) and cook as above. Stir in some fresh coriander at the end and serve with couscous.

• Make a little white sauce (the recipe on p74, leaving out the cheese) and pour it over the fish, adding a few frozen prawns and some chopped parsley if you have some. Heat through and season to taste with lemon juice. Serve with mash as a deconstructed fish pie.

• Cook one side of the fish in a pan with a little oil or butter, then turn it over and top it with a sliced fresh tomato and some grated Cheddar. Flash under a hot grill until the cheese is melted and bubbling.

• Make a cod, bacon and sweetcorn chowder. Chop half an onion and fry with 2 chopped slices of streaky bacon until the bacon is beginning to crisp. Stir in 1 teaspoon of flour and 225ml of milk. Bring to the boil and add a cubed fish steak, 4 tablespoons of sweetcorn kernels and 2 diced cooked potatoes. Simmer for 3–4 minutes until the fish is cooked.

• Mix 2 heaped tablespoons of yoghurt, $1/_2$ a teaspoon of curry paste and a squeeze of lemon. Marinate the fish for 15 minutes then grill. Serve with rice and/or salad.

REALLY EASY THAI GREEN FISH CURRY
Serves 1

Thai curry devotees may regard this as a bit of a cop-out but it takes a fraction of the time of the authentic version and is surprisingly really tasty.

1 frozen skinless, boneless white fish fillet (about 110g–125g)

1 tbsp vegetable oil

Half a bunch of spring onions, trimmed and sliced, or a small onion, peeled and roughly chopped

1 clove of garlic, peeled and crushed

2–3 tsp Thai green curry paste or Thai green curry powder

1/4–1/3 of a tin of coconut milk or 150ml coconut milk made from coconut powder

1 tbsp of plain yoghurt (optional but nice)

50g frozen peas

2 tsp lime or lemon juice, preferably freshly squeezed

1 heaped tbsp fresh chopped coriander (optional but good)

If you remember or have time, take the fish out of the freezer about 15 minutes before you start cooking so it's easier to cut. Heat the oil in a saucepan, add the spring onion and cook over a low heat for a couple of minutes until beginning to soften. Add the crushed garlic and stir in the curry paste or powder, then pour in the coconut milk and yoghurt and stir again. Heat through while you cut the fish into cubes (easiest with scissors) and add it and the peas to the coconut milk. Bring to the boil then turn the heat down and simmer until cooked (about 2–3 minutes). Stir in the lime or lemon juice and fresh coriander, cook for another minute then serve with rice.

EXTEND FOR A FRIEND
This is actually an impressive dish to make for friends. Increase quantities to 2 tablespoons of oil, 1 bunch spring onions, 2 cloves garlic, 2 tablespoons of Thai paste or curry powder, a whole tin of coconut milk, 500g fish, a mug of frozen peas, 2 tablespoons lime juice and 3 heaped tablespoons of coriander. Chuck in a few frozen prawns too.

TRY THIS TOO...
Instead of the fish you could make this with about 150g of cooked chicken, cut into cubes.

£ WITH THE LEFTOVER COCONUT MILK
• Make the Tunaco Fish Soup on p108.
• Stir it into a curry paste.
• Whiz some up with mango pulp for an exotic smoothie.

Stir-fries are great student food – fast and healthy – but they can be pricey too, particularly if you buy those ready-made stir-in sauces. For a basic stir-fry stick to the cheaper stir-fry mixes and use soy sauce.

BASIC, SIMPLE STIR-FRY

If you want to serve rice with it; cook it beforehand (see p86).

2 tbsp oil
1/2 a small bag of stir-fry vegetables (about 150g)
A cooked chicken thigh, skin removed and cut into thin strips or 75g of cashew nuts (optional)
2 tbsp light soy sauce

Heat a wok or large frying pan until it begins to smoke. Pour in the oil and immediately tip in the vegetables and the chicken or nuts, if using. Cook for a couple of minutes, moving them about continually so they don't burn. Add about 3 tablespoons of water and cook until evaporated. Add the soy sauce and cook for a few seconds more. Taste, adding more soy if you think it needs it. Serve up.

£ WHAT TO DO WITH THE REST OF THE STIR-FRY VEG

If they're absolutely fresh – i.e. you've just bought them and they have a couple of days to go to the 'eat-by' date you could use them to make a salad with the Bang Bang dressing on p49. Otherwise you could use them in a spicy Asian-style soup (see p53).

SWEET AND SOUR CHICKEN (OR TURKEY)
Serves 1–2

A homemade sweet and sour sauce is surprisingly good.

2 tbsp soy sauce
1 chicken or turkey breast or fillet, cut into fine strips
2 tbsp oil
1 small carrot, peeled and cut into thin strips
1/2 a red or green pepper, de-seeded and cut into thin strips
1/2 a bunch of spring onions, trimmed and finely sliced or a small onion, peeled and finely sliced
1 clove of garlic, peeled and crushed
1/2 a small (227g) tin of pineapple pieces in natural juice
1 tbsp tomato ketchup
1 tsp lemon juice or vinegar if needed

Put 1 tbsp of the soy sauce in a bowl, add the chicken or turkey strips and mix together. Heat the oil in a frying pan or wok. Add the chicken, carrot and pepper and stir-fry for about 3 minutes. Add the spring onions and garlic and fry for another minute. Drain the pineapple, reserving the juice. Add half the pineapple and all the juice to the stir-fry, along with the ketchup and remaining soy sauce. Taste and add the lemon juice or vinegar if needed. Serve with rice or noodles.

TRY THIS TOO...

You could also make this with belly pork, pre-cooked for a few minutes in boiling water then drained and deep fried (see below).

£ LEFTOVER PINEAPPLE?

Eat the rest of the pineapple for breakfast with some low-fat fromage frais, yoghurt or add it to a fruit salad (see p80).

CRISPY PORK AND GREENS WITH SPAGHETTI NOODLES

Ultra-cheap belly pork lends itself really well to stir-frying, but you need to pre-cook it first to make it tender. Supermarkets tend to sell it in packs big enough for two, so prepare it, use what you need and use the rest in another recipe (see leftovers, below). Note the use of spaghetti as noodles – a big money saver!

450g belly pork strips
A small handful of spaghetti (about 50g)
100ml vegetable oil
1 small clove of garlic
A small lump of ginger, peeled and finely chopped or grated or $1/2$ tsp ginger paste
$1/4$ of a spring cabbage or a small head of spring greens, trimmed of any tough stalks, shredded and rinsed under cold water
1–2 tbsp soy sauce plus extra for serving

With a sharp knife cut away any rind on the belly pork strips, then cut them across into thin slices (about 6 to a strip). Put them in a saucepan, cover with cold water and slowly bring to the boil. Spoon off any froth and simmer very gently for 15–20 minutes. Drain and cool for 10 minutes or so. Break the spaghetti in half and cook for just under the time recommended on the pack.

Drain, reserving some of the cooking water, and rinse in cold water. Heat the oil in a wok for about 3 minutes until hot, then fry the pork pieces until crisp, turning them with a slotted spoon (about 4 minutes). Pour the fat in the wok away, except for about 2 tablespoons. Add the garlic, ginger and cabbage to the pan and stir-fry for a few seconds then return the pork to the pan. Add 1 tablespoon of soy sauce and a couple of tablespoons of the pasta cooking water and stir-fry for 2 or 3 minutes. Add the cooked, drained spaghetti and heat through. Check the seasoning, adding extra soy or a dash of hot pepper sauce if needed.

£ LEFTOVERS

You could add the remaining belly pork to a lentil or bean stew (see p69).

TOMATO+CUCUMBER+ PEPPER+CELERY+ ONION+CARROT+APPLE

Most student fridges, I think it's fair to say, don't have a salad drawer crammed with fabulous ingredients. In my experience the contents are most likely to be tomatoes, peppers and cucumber with perhaps an onion and a couple of carrots in the veg rack, and a still unwrapped bag of apples lying around on a work surface. Add a bunch of celery, a few other inexpensive ingredients, and you can make any one of the following easy salads.

CARROT AND APPLE SLAW

Peel and grate a medium-sized carrot and put into a bowl. Add half an apple, grated and tossed in one tablespoon of lemon juice (to stop it going brown). You could also chuck in one or more of the following: a couple of finely shredded spring onions, some finely sliced celery or green pepper, a few raisins or sultanas or some cashew nuts if you have some. Add two tablespoons of sunflower oil or light olive oil, toss together and season to taste with salt and pepper and more lemon juice if it needs it. (You could also spice it up with a teaspoon of Moroccan Spice Mix – see p19)

TOMATO AND ONION (OR PLAIN TOMATO) SALAD

Slice a couple of ripe tomatoes and put them in a bowl. Take a couple of slices off a mild onion (preferably a red onion, or a large Spanish one), break it up into rings and add to the tomato, along with a little chopped parsley if you have some. Pour over a couple of spoonfuls of Budget Salad Dressing (see opposite) and mix well together. Leave for 5–10 minutes for the flavours to infuse.

TZATZIKI
(pronounced 'zatziki')

A simple Greek cucumber salad, similar to Indian raita.

Cut off a quarter of a cucumber, peel it and then grate it coarsely into a sieve or colander. Squeeze the grated cucumber with your hands to extract as much liquid as possible and transfer to a bowl. Add one crushed clove of garlic or a tablespoon of finely chopped onion, two heaped tablespoons of plain unsweetened yoghurt, a few drops of lemon juice or vinegar, one tablespoon of oil and a little chopped fresh mint if you have some. Mix. Good with spicy sausages or burgers – unless you're a veggie, of course – or with fried courgettes.

CHEESE, CELERY AND APPLE SALAD

Wash, trim and slice 2 sticks of celery. Quarter and chop a small apple and sprinkle the pieces with lemon juice. Add a good chunk of Cheddar cheese, cut into small cubes. You could also add a few leaves from a crunchy lettuce like a little gem or a small handful of walnuts if you have some. Mix 1 heaped tablespoon of yoghurt with 1 heaped tablespoon of mayo and mix with the salad. Check the seasoning, adding salt, pepper and more lemon juice to taste. Good with cold ham.

ARAB SALAD

Most middle eastern and Turkish restaurants offer something like this simple fresh salad which is almost more like a salsa. Peel, de-seed and finely chop a $1/4$ of a cucumber and place in a bowl. Add 1–2 chopped ripe tomatoes (depending on size), $1/2$ a small red pepper and 1–2 finely sliced spring onions, or a couple of slices of mild onion, all finely chopped. Whisk together 1 dessertspoon of lemon juice with $2^1/2$ dessertspoons of sunflower or light olive oil and season with salt and a pinch of chilli pepper and/or cumin if you have some. Add to the chopped vegetables (with 1 heaped tablespoon of chopped parsley if available) and toss together.

CRUDITES

Cut all or any of the following – cucumber, carrot, celery and peppers – into strips and serve with garlic mayo, made by crushing $1/2$ a clove of garlic into 1 heaped tablespoon of mayonnaise mixed with 1 heaped tablespoon of low-fat yoghurt. Or use the Bang Bang dressing on p49.

BUDGET SALAD DRESSING

2 tsp wine vinegar or lemon juice
$2^1/2$ tbsp sunflower oil or, better still, olive oil
$1/2$ a clove of garlic, peeled and crushed (optional)
Salt, pepper and a pinch of sugar

Put all the ingredients in a jam jar and shake well together, or whisk in a bowl with a fork. If you have some Dijon mustard add $1/4$ of a teaspoon of that too.

Whether you're veggie or not, vegetables provide a good, cheap starting point for a number of different meals.

MUSHROOMS

As well as being dead tasty, mushrooms are really low in calories and contain a useful amount of protein. You can buy big packs very cheaply – or buy them loose.

THOROUGHLY VERSATILE MUSHROOM AND BACON SAUCE
Serves 1–2

A cheap and easy sauce that goes well with rice or pasta. It can be used as a topping for toast or baked potatoes and makes a good pancake filling. Use small white or chestnut mushrooms, rather than the big flat ones which will turn your sauce a dirty grey.

2 tbsp vegetable, sunflower or olive oil
2 rashers of back bacon or 3–4 rashers of streaky, rind removed and chopped
1 small onion or 1/2 medium onion, peeled and roughly chopped
1 small clove of garlic, peeled and crushed (optional)
125g button or chestnut mushrooms, rinsed and sliced
1/4–1/2 tsp paprika
1 tsp plain flour
100ml milk
3 tbsp double or whipping cream or crème fraîche
Ground black pepper and lemon juice to taste
1 tbsp chopped parsley (optional)

Heat the oil in a small pan and add the chopped bacon. Fry until it begins to brown then add the chopped onion, turn the heat down and cook for about 5–6 minutes until the onion starts to soften. Add the garlic and mushrooms, stir and cook for another 3 minutes. Stir in the paprika and flour, cook for another minute then pour in the milk and bring to the boil. Turn the heat down, add the cream and simmer for another 2–3 minutes. Season to taste with pepper and a good squeeze of lemon and stir in the parsley, if using.

£ SPARE MUSHROOMS?
• Add them to your fry-up.
• Fry in a little oil and butter and use as an omelette filling (see p72) or add to scrambled eggs.
• Make a Brie and Mushroom Melt (see p76).
• Make a raw mushroom salad with chopped spring onions and a little Budget Salad Dressing (see p61). Only do this when they're really fresh.
• Make a pilau with rice (see p51).

£ LEFTOVER CREAM
You could use any leftover cream for other creamy cheese sauces, or with porridge, or as a topping for fruit.

CAULIFLOWER

One good sized cauliflower will make a cauli cheese, a veggie curry and some tasty fritters like these.

CAULIFLOWER PAKORAS 🌱 Serves 1–2

A simple snack that with some raita (p115), fresh coriander chutney (p115) and naan, pitta bread or chapatti (p114) makes a meal.

- 75g (½ a mug) gram (chickpea) flour
- ½ tsp cumin seeds
- ½ tsp turmeric or mild curry powder
- ¼ tsp salt plus a little extra for sprinkling
- ¼ tsp baking powder (optional)
- ⅓ of a medium cauliflower, broken up into florets weighing about 125g in total
- Vegetable oil for deep-frying (about 250ml)§

Put the flour in a bowl with the cumin seeds, turmeric or curry powder, salt and baking powder. Pour in just enough water to make a thick batter, beating it with a wooden spoon as you go to keep the mixture smooth. (You'll need about 100–125ml). Cut the florets into even-sized pieces so they cook at the same time. Heat a wok and pour in enough oil to give you a depth of about 4 cm. Heat for about 4 minutes. Tip some of the cauliflower into the batter and turn it with a spoon so that each piece is completely covered. Extract a piece, shaking off any excess batter, and drop it in the oil. It should start sizzling immediately. If not, heat the oil a bit longer. Fry the cauliflower in batches a few pieces at the time, turning them half way through, until nicely browned. Transfer them to a plate as you cook them.

TRY THIS TOO...

Other veg that taste good in this batter are sliced courgettes and aubergines, peeled and sliced sweet potato and onion rings.

CAULIFLOWER CHEESE 🌱

Cut half a small cauliflower into florets and boil or steam it until you can easily pierce it with a sharp knife (about 8 minutes). Drain, put into an ovenproof dish and pour over some cheese sauce (see p74). Sprinkle with a little extra cheese and brown under the grill.

CAULIFLOWER AND POTATO CURRY 🌱

Fry an onion in a couple of tablespoons of oil until soft. Add a crushed clove of garlic, a teaspoon of mild curry paste or powder and, if you have one, a finely chopped de-seeded chilli and stir. Tip in some cooked chopped cauliflower and some cooked cubed potato and a few peas. Keep frying over a moderate heat until heated through (about 2–3 minutes) adding a splash of water if the veg start catching on the pan. Season with salt and a squeeze of lemon juice. Add some chopped fresh coriander if you have some.

PEPPERS

Peppers are incredibly versatile and a great source of vitamin C. It's usually better value to buy them in a mixed bag rather than individually. Here are a few things to do with them.

RIDICULOUSLY EASY ROAST PEPPERS 🌱

Although I wouldn't normally advocate turning on your oven for one meal you can make a big batch of roast peppers and use them all week – as a veg, in salads, sandwiches or pitta bread or in pasta sauces. (To save fuel, cook them when you're roasting something else like a chicken or baking a crumble.)

3 tbsp olive oil or other cooking oil
4 large peppers, quartered with the stalk, pith and seeds removed

Preheat the oven to 190C/375F/Gas 5. Take a large roasting tin and pour in the oil. Tip in the peppers, mix them with the oil then lay them out in a single layer. Season lightly with salt and pepper and bake for about 50 minutes or until the peppers are soft and well caramelised.

PIEDMONTESE PEPPERS 🌱

There's a great version of the above recipe called Piedmontese Peppers. You need to use red rather than green peppers, halved rather than quartered and olive oil rather than vegetable oil. Pour a couple of tablespoons in the dish, lay out the halved peppers as described above and put a slice of fresh tomato, a couple of thin slices of garlic and an anchovy, if you like, in each half. Trickle over another 3–4 tablespoons of oil and bake on a slightly lower setting (180C/350F/Gas 4) for an hour.

The oil picks up a wonderful garlicky, peppery flavour. Great with soft cheese and crusty bread.

OTHER GOOD THINGS TO DO WITH PEPPERS

Both fresh and frozen peppers are great additions to stir-fries, salads, stews and pasta sauces. See Hot Penne with Red Peppers and 'Fake Feta' (p40), Sweet and Sour Chicken (on p58), the salads on pp60-61 and Pork, Pepper and Potato Goulash on p100.

ONIONS

You've probably pretty well always got a few onions to hand, or can easily walk down the street and buy them. Here's a couple of good things to do with them.

ONION MARMALADE ✤
Enough for 3–4 helpings

Posh delis would charge a fortune for this onion chutney. You can make it for a fraction of that. Great with sausages, or in cheese or ham sandwiches.

3 tbsp vegetable oil
3–4 onions, peeled and thinly sliced (about 400g) red onions are nicest
A small slice of butter (about 15g)
1 tsp sugar
Salt, ground black pepper and vinegar to taste

Heat a large frying pan or wok and add the oil. Fry the onions over a moderately high heat, stirring them occasionally until soft and well browned (about 10 minutes). Add the butter and sugar, turn the heat down a little and continue to fry, stirring, for another 5–10 minutes. Season to taste with salt, pepper and a little vinegar if you think it needs sharpening up. Keep any leftovers in the fridge.

FRENCH ONION SOUP ✤
Enough for 2–3 helpings

Follow the above recipe until the onions are cooked, then stir in a teaspoon of plain flour and add 450ml (2 mugs) of stock made with 2 level teaspoons of Marmite. Bring to the boil and simmer for 10 minutes. Season to taste with salt, pepper and vinegar if needed. Pour into bowls and lay some baked crostini (see below) on top. Cover with a layer of grated Cheddar and flash under the grill.

TO MAKE CROSTINI

Cut thin slices of a day-old French baguette or ciabatta and bake them in a moderate oven (180/350F/Gas 4) for about 15 minutes until brown and crisp. They can be used as a base for paté and spreads too.

BAKED BEANS

Despite the title of this book and its predecessors, I have nothing against baked beans. They're a good wholesome food that provides protein, fibre and some useful minerals such as iron. Here are various ways of enjoying them....

CHILLI BAKED BEANS
🌱 Serves 1

1 tbsp oil
1/2 a medium onion, peeled and roughly chopped
1 clove of garlic, peeled and crushed (optional)
1/2 a red pepper, de-seeded and cut into strips or a handful of frozen peppers
1–1 1/2 tsp mild chilli powder or 1 tsp paprika
Half a 400g tin of baked beans
Fresh parsley, chopped (optional)

Heat the oil in a saucepan or small frying pan and fry the onion over a moderately high heat for about 5 minutes until it begins to brown at the edges. Turn the heat down a bit and add the garlic, if using, and peppers. Stir and cook for a couple of minutes. Add the chilli power and beans, stir and cook for another couple of minutes until heated through, adding a little water if the sauce seems too thick. Add the parsley, if using. Good with wholemeal toast, sausages or a baked potato.

£ WHAT TO DO WITH THE OTHER HALF OF THE TIN...
CURRY BEANS 🌱

Fry a small or 1/2 a medium onion as described above, add a clove of crushed garlic and 1/2–1 teaspoons of curry paste or 1–1 1/2 teaspoons of Moroccan Spice Mix (see p19). Tip in half a tin of beans and heat through. Add a squeeze of lemon or a few drops of wine vinegar and a heaped teaspoon of fresh coriander or a handful of fresh spinach leaves. (Or some frozen leaf spinach, cooked, well drained and squeezed dry.) Serve with rice.

£ OR THIS...
BAKED BEAN AND BACON MELT

Cut up 4 streaky bacon rashers into pieces and fry them in 1 tablespoon of oil until almost crisp. Add 4 finely sliced spring onions and stir-fry for a minute or two. Tip in half a tin of beans and heat through for a couple of minutes. Make a slice of wholemeal toast and butter lightly. Season the beans with black pepper, add a handful (about 25-30g) of grated strong Cheddar then, once it starts melting, spoon the beans over the toast.

RED KIDNEY BEANS

You probably bought them to go in a Chilli Con Carne (p43). Here's what to do with the rest. See also Winter Soup (p46).

RED BEAN AND WHITE CHEESE SALAD ♦
Serves 1

2 tsp lemon juice
5 tsp sunflower oil or light olive oil
$\frac{1}{2}$ a 400g tin of red kidney beans, drained and rinsed
1–2 spring onions, trimmed and finely sliced, or a finely chopped slice of onion
50g Caerphilly, white Cheshire or Wensleydale cheese, cut into small cubes
A heaped tbsp finely chopped parsley and a little mint if you have some
Salt and ground black pepper

Spoon the lemon juice and sunflower oil into a bowl, season with salt and pepper and whisk together with a fork. Add the kidney beans, sliced or chopped onion, cheese and parsley and/or mint, if using, and toss together.

MEXICAN-STYLE RE-FRIED BEANS ♦

Heat 2 tablespoons of vegetable oil in a frying pan and add a small finely chopped onion. Fry over a moderate heat for about 4–5 minutes till beginning to soften. Add a clove of crushed garlic, $\frac{1}{2}$ teaspoon of chilli powder and a chopped fresh, or tinned tomato, or a couple of tablespoons of passata, stir and cook for another minute. Add $\frac{1}{2}$ a tin of drained and rinsed red kidney beans then turn the heat down, cover the pan and cook for 3–4 minutes. Take the pan off the heat and mash the beans roughly with a fork. Season to taste with salt, lemon juice and a pinch of cumin if you have some and stir in a tablespoon of chopped fresh coriander. Cool for 10 minutes or so then use the mixture to stuff a pitta bread or wrap together with some sliced cucumber, tomato and onion.

CHICKPEAS

Being a good source of protein, chickpeas are a useful addition to veggie stews, curries and couscous.

VERY EASY CHICKPEA CURRY 🌿
Serves 1 + leftovers

As simple as a plate of spaghetti; I like it with fresh tomatoes when they're ripe enough, but you can easily use tinned ones.

2 tbsp vegetable or sunflower oil
1 medium onion, peeled and roughly chopped
1 clove of garlic, peeled and crushed or finely chopped
1/2 tsp mild curry paste or powder
3 medium-sized tomatoes, skinned and roughly chopped plus 1 tsp tomato paste or 1/2 a 400g tin of tomatoes
A 400g tin of chickpeas, drained and rinsed or 250g freshly cooked chickpeas (see p116)

2 tbsp chopped fresh coriander or a handful of fresh spinach leaves or frozen leaf spinach
Salt

Heat the oil in a frying pan and fry the onion for about 4–5 minutes until soft. Stir in the garlic and curry paste, or powder, and fry for a few seconds, then tip in the chopped tomatoes and tomato paste, if using. Add half a mug of water, bring to the boil then simmer until the tomatoes begin to break down. Add the chickpeas and leave on a low heat for about 5–6 minutes, adding a little more water if they get too dry. Chuck in the coriander or spinach and cook for another 2 minutes. Add salt to taste. You could serve this with a dollop of yoghurt and some pitta bread or naan.

£ LEFTOVER CHICKPEAS?

Mash any leftover chickpeas and use them to fill a pitta bread.

TRY THIS TOO...
CHEAT'S HUMMUS 🌿

If you have a blender or food processor you can also make an easy and economical hummus with a tin of chickpeas. Drain and rinse the chickpeas and whiz them in a blender till you have a thick paste. Add a clove of crushed garlic, 1 1/2 tablespoons of tahini, 1 tablespoons of yoghurt, 1 1/2 tablespoons of lemon juice, 2 tablespoons of water and 1/4 of a teaspoon each of ground cumin and salt and whiz again. Adjust the seasoning, adding a little extra water if the hummus seems too thick.

LENTILS

There's something about the word lentil that's a massive turn-off. But they're surprisingly tasty if you allow yourself to like them. They're also a great source of protein and iron.

SPINACH, LENTIL AND CORIANDER SOUP 🍃
Enough for 2 helpings

This might sound weird but it's a great combination.

2 tbsp vegetable oil
1 small onion or half a medium onion, peeled and roughly chopped
$1/2$–$3/4$ tsp cumin
$1/2$ x 400g tin of lentils, drained and rinsed
100g frozen leaf spinach or a large handful of fresh spinach leaves with any tough stalks removed
A few roughly chopped coriander stalks
350ml stock made with 2 tsp vegetable bouillon powder
2–3 tsp lemon juice
2 tbsp plain yoghurt plus extra if you want for serving
Salt and ground black pepper
Coriander leaves for garnish

Heat the oil in a large saucepan and fry the onion over a moderate heat for about 5–6 minutes until beginning to brown. Add the cumin, lentils, spinach and coriander stalks, stir then pour in two-thirds of the stock. Bring to the boil and simmer for about 5 minutes or until the spinach has completely defrosted. Whiz up the soup with a blender until smooth and return to the pan. Add the lemon juice, yoghurt and as much stock as you need to get a nice thin consistency. Check the seasoning, adding salt, pepper and more cumin if you think it needs it. Spoon into a bowl or bowls, add an extra swirl of yoghurt if you want to pretty it up and sprinkle with the coriander leaves.

£ LEFTOVER LENTILS?

• Fry up some finely chopped onion, carrot and celery, add the lentils and a little Marmite stock (see p93) and simmer for 5 minutes. Serve with grilled or fried sausages.
• Fry some onion and garlic, add a pinch of paprika and stir in some crispy-fried pork (see p59). Add the lentils and heat through.

Even if you're on a budget, try to buy decent eggs. By decent I mean free-range and fresh. Good for the chicken as well as for you.

MEAL 1
FULL FRY-UP

(Egg, bacon, sausage and tomato – 1–2 eggs)

You probably know how to cook a fry-up but here are a few tips. Heat the pan and the oil for at least a couple of minutes before you start. Buy small chipolata sausages (they cook more quickly) and get them on first. Next the tomatoes: cut them in half, season with salt and pepper and put them in the pan, cut side down. Turn them after about 3 minutes.

If you're using cheap bacon it helps to microwave it briefly first to get rid of the goo that otherwise oozes into the pan. To do this lay 2–3 rashers on a plate, cover loosely with a sheet of kitchen towel and cook on HIGH for a minute. Then pat them dry before you fry them – they'll be crisper. Crack the egg(s) into a saucer before you add them to the pan – you're less likely to break the yolk. Tilt the pan and spoon the hot fat over them as you cook them to set the yolks. If you only have a medium-sized frying pan cook the sausages, tomatoes and bacon, then put them aside on a warm plate. Wipe the pan, add a little more oil or oil and butter and cook the eggs.

MEAL 2
SOFT-BOILED EGG AND 'SOLDIERS' ☙
(1–2 eggs)

Best to start with the eggs at room temperature if you can so they don't crack. Bring a small pan of water to the boil. Place each egg in a spoon and lower it carefully into the water so that the water covers the eggs. Boil for $3^1/_2$–4 minutes for medium eggs and 4–$4^1/_2$ minutes for large eggs. Meanwhile, toast and butter one or two slices of wholegrain bread and cut into long strips. Dunk the 'soldiers' in the runny egg yolk. Mmmm.

MEAL 3
EGG MAYO AND CRESS SANDWICH OR ROLL ☙
(2 hard-boiled eggs)

Follow recipe as above but carry on boiling eggs for 10 minutes in total. Remove the eggs and transfer them to a bowl of cold water to cool down. After 3 or 4 minutes crack the shells gently against a hard surface and peel off the shell under running water. Put the peeled eggs in a bowl and chop roughly with a knife. Add a heaped tablespoon of mayo and a little chopped onion, or spring onion, and season with salt and pepper. Use to fill a sandwich, pitta bread or roll, topping the egg with a handful of cress leaves. (Use the rest of the cress next time you make a salad.)

MEAL 4
SCRAMBLED EGGS 🌱
(2 large or 3 medium eggs)

Put a non-stick saucepan over a low heat. Add a slice of butter (about 15–20g) and melt gently. Break 3 medium or 2 large eggs into a bowl. Add a few drops of milk season with salt and pepper and beat the mixture with a fork until the yolks are amalgamated with the whites. Tip the eggs into the pan and cook, stirring, over a very low heat until the mixture thickens into a rich, golden mass (about 3–5 minutes). If you want to add other ingredients e.g. ham or fried mushrooms add them just as the mixture is thickening. Serve on hot buttered toast.

MEAL 5
HAM OR CHEESE OMELETTE
(2–3 large eggs)

2–3 large eggs, preferably free-range
A good slice of butter (about 15g)
1 thick or 2 thin slices of lean ham, cut into strips **or** a handful (30–40g) grated Cheddar cheese
Salt and pepper

Crack, season and beat the eggs as described above but adding a splash of water rather than milk. Heat a small non-stick frying pan until moderately hot and add the butter. When the sizzling has died down pour the beaten egg into the pan. Working quickly, keep lifting the egg up and away from the edges of the pan so that the liquid egg runs underneath. When the base of the omelette is just firm, scatter the ham or cheese over the surface. Cook for a few seconds more then ease a spatula under one side of the omelette, roll it up over the filling and tip it onto a plate.

MEAL 6
FRITTATA
(4 large or 5 medium eggs)

A frittata is essentially the same as an omelette, except that it has more filling and is open rather than rolled. It's a brilliant way to use up odd veg or other bits and pieces you find in the fridge. The leftovers can be eaten cold the next day.

2 tbsp cooking oil
2–3 slices of bacon or ham chopped
A small onion, peeled and chopped or a trimmed and finely sliced leek or 4 spring onions, trimmed and finely sliced
1/2 a small green or red pepper
3–4 cooked potatoes, cut into cubes
Any leftover (but not whiskery) green veg, e.g. peas, beans or broccoli (optional)
4 large or 5 medium eggs, preferably free-range
Salt and pepper

Heat the oil in a small to medium-sized frying pan and fry the bacon pieces for a couple of minutes until the fat starts to run. Add the onion and peppers and fry until beginning to soften (about 4 minutes), then add the potatoes and any leftover veg. Turn the heat down and cook over a low heat for about 5 minutes until the contents of the pan are thoroughly heated through, turning them occasionally. Crack the eggs into a bowl, beat lightly with a fork and season with salt and pepper. Turn the heat up and pour the egg evenly over the bacon and vegetables. With a fork, lift the edges of the frittata as it cooks to allow the liquid egg to run over the base of the pan. Leave it to cook for another 3–4 minutes while you turn on the grill and then put the pan briefly under the grill (not too close) to brown the top of the frittata. (If you don't have a grill, slide the frittata onto a plate, then flip it back into the pan to cook the other side.)

Eat half the frittata hot and save half for the next day. (You can use it to stuff large rolls or pitta bread.)

OTHER THINGS YOU CAN MAKE WITH EGGS
Extra Creamy Carbonara (p39) and Egg-Fried Rice (p86).

74 CLEVER THINGS TO DO WITH CHEESE

WHAT TO DO WITH A BLOCK OF CHEDDAR...

...or Lancashire for that matter. Cheese, especially Cheddar, can take up a good chunk of your weekly budget so you need to both watch out what you're paying for it, (see p16) and make it last. The only way to protect it from the scavenging fridge raiders in your kitchen is to divide it into portions when you first unwrap it and re-wrap in foil (so the fridge raiders can't spot what it is). A normal portion is 50g – about a quarter to a fifth of a small block, 25g if you're using it as a topping. Here's what to do with it.

MAKE A CHEESE SAUCE
'THE CLASSIC METHOD'

To make enough for 1 helping – melt a tablespoon (15g) of butter gently in a small non-stick saucepan ((if you haven't got soft-enough butter or scales, most packs of butter are marked in 25g portions, so you need just over half of one of these portions). Stir in a tablespoon of plain flour and cook over a low heat for about a minute. Take the pan off the heat and gradually add 150ml of whole or semi-skimmed milk, bit by bit, stirring between each addition. Bring the sauce to the boil, turn the heat right down and simmer for 5 minutes until the sauce is thick and smooth. Take off the heat and add 25g of mature Cheddar or Lancashire cheese and season with salt and pepper. To make the sauce slightly lighter add a tablespoon or two of any pasta or vegetable cooking water you have. To make it richer add a couple of tablespoons of cream. Use it to cover freshly cooked pasta shapes like penne or rigatoni for a macaroni cheese (it'll make enough to cover 75g dried weight), or make a Cauliflower Cheese (see p63). Just scatter over another 25g of cheese and brown under the grill.

'THE ALL-IN-ONE METHOD'

This way the ingredients all go in the pan at once, which obviously saves time. You will need a small balloon whisk though. Put the butter, milk and flour (same quantities as the above recipe) in a pan and bring gradually to the boil, whisking energetically. Turn the heat down and simmer for 5 minutes then turn off the heat and add the cheese as described above. (Be careful not to carry on cooking a sauce once you've added the cheese – it makes it stringy.)

MAKE A CRUSTY TOPPING

Use grated cheese to make a tasty topping for a piece of fish or a veggie bake. Just scatter or press it on and then brown under a hot grill until bubbling and crisp. About 25g should be enough for this.

MAKE A SNACK
SARNIES AND TOASTIES

Cheese obviously makes great sarnies or filled rolls. Cheddar goes particularly well with sweet pickle and other chutneys, or cram in as much salad veg as you can. Grating it bulks it out – makes you feel you've got more cheese!

PAN-FRIED CHEESE AND ONION TOASTIE

If you haven't got a sandwich maker or double-sided electric contact grill, simply spread one side of each piece of bread with butter, or butter-based spread. Lay one piece buttered-side down and top with half the cheese, add thin slices of onion and/or a slice of ham, add the rest of the cheese and place the other piece of bread on top, buttered side upwards. Heat a small frying pan without any oil, lay the sandwich in the pan and cook for about $1\frac{1}{2}$ minutes, pressing it down firmly with a spatula then carefully turn the sandwich over and cook the other side. Keep flipping it over until both sides are nicely browned and the cheese melted and gooey.

BEST-EVER CHEESE ON TOAST (BUDGET VERSION) 🍁

A foolproof way of making cheese on toast that stops the cheese going stringy, or the toast going soggy. (Readers of my previous books will spot the quantity of cheese has been reduced. Well this is the budget version....)

50g mature Cheddar or
　Lancashire cheese, grated
1 tsp flour
$\frac{1}{2}$ tsp Dijon mustard or brown
　sauce (optional)
2 tbsp milk
A couple of slices of wholemeal
　bread

Put all the ingredients except the toast in a saucepan and bring slowly to the boil, stirring. Toast the bread. Pour the melted cheese over the toast.

MAKE A SALAD

There's a good one on p61.

HAVE A SNACK

A hunk of cheese and an apple. And maybe a few raisins. Or if you're feeling hungrier, a crispbread sandwich – two slices of Scandinavian-style crispbread (I like Ryvita Multigrain) with thinly sliced cheese.

BRIE

Brie is one of the cheapest cheeses. It goes particularly well with grapes and summer fruit like cherries and raspberries, or have it hot with mushrooms, aubergine or roasted peppers (see p64).

BRIE AND MUSHROOM MELT ♥ Serves 1

1 tbsp oil
A little butter
100g mushrooms, rinsed and sliced
Half a small baguette or a quarter of a longer one
50g of brie, thinly sliced
Salt and pepper

Preheat your grill. Heat a small pan and add the oil, then, after a few seconds, the butter. When the butter has melted, tip in the mushrooms and stir-fry for 2–3 minutes. Take off the heat and season with salt and pepper. Split the baguette and put the bottom slice on a grill pan, cut-side upwards. Pile the mushrooms on top and cover with slices of brie. Grill until the brie melts. Put on a plate and top with the other piece of baguette, pressing down well. (You could, of course, simply make this on toast rather than as a sandwich.)

TRY THIS TOO...
Instead of mushrooms you could use roasted peppers (see p64) or crisp, fried streaky bacon.

QUARK

My favourite low-fat soft cheese: much better – and cheaper – than Philadelphia! Use as you'd use soft goats' cheese or try the dip below.

LOW-FAT CHEESE AND ONION DIP ♥

Mix half a 250g packet of Quark with 4–5 tablespoons of semi-skimmed milk, add a couple of tablespoons of finely-chopped onion, or spring onion and a small clove of garlic (if you like things garlicky). Season with salt and a dash of hot pepper sauce (if you like things spicy too). Perfect for dunking in raw veg, such as carrots and peppers.

STILTON AND OTHER BLUE CHEESE

Blue cheese isn't to everyone's taste but a little goes a long way, particularly if you stretch it with butter, cream or fromage frais.

BLUE CHEESE BUTTER ✿

Great with baked potatoes or – if you really feel like treating yourself – steak. Mash equal amounts of blue cheese and butter together and season with ground black pepper.

MAKE A BLUE CHEESE DRESSING ✿

Replace one of the tablespoons of oil in the Budget Salad Dressing on p61 with cream and then crumble in 25g of blue cheese. Great with iceberg lettuce.

MAKE A REALLY WICKED BLUE CHEESE SAUCE ✿

Melt 75g of Dolcelatte (mild gorgonzola) in a pan with 1 tablespoon of double cream. Heat very gently, stirring until the cheese has melted. Add another 2–3 tablespoons of cream until the mixture develops the texture of a sauce. Season to taste with black pepper and a squeeze of lemon. Great poured over lightly cooked cauliflower, broccoli or leeks.

CRUMBLY WHITE CHEESE

Such as Caerphilly, Wensleydale, white Cheshire. Great for crumbling over salads or pasta dishes – use as a substitute for the more expensive Feta (see Hot Penne with Red Peppers and Fake Feta on p40) and the Red Bean and White Cheese Salad on p67).

FROMAGE FRAIS

Technically a cheese, but more useful as a low-fat, low-cost cream-substitute. Terrific with strawberries and raspberries.

GOATS' CHEESE

Comes into the treat category, but if you're allergic to cow's milk it's a well justified one. Goats' cheese is great with all things salady and herby. Try the Grilled Goats' Cheese Salad with Garlic Toasts on p127.

Fresh fruit is one of the foods that tends to go by the board when you're budgeting. Probably because a lot of it is expensive and it's often unripe and unappetising. Or you simply don't know what to do with it. But, as you don't need me to remind you, it should be an integral part of your 5-a-day regime.

The solution is to make it more of a treat. Cook it or squish it, sweeten it, then mix or whiz it with yoghurt, fromage frais, custard or even cream which is one of the great unheralded food bargains; not just indulgence – it makes it go further.

REAL FRUIT YOGHURTS

Don't know if you've ever noticed how little fruit there is in a cheap fruit yoghurt? Scarcely any in some cases. You can easily remedy that by mixing in crushed or cooked fruit such as this scrummy compote.

BRAMLEY APPLE AND BLACKBERRY COMPOTE 🍁
Makes enough for 4 helpings

Fruits that make good fruit compotes are Bramley apples, rhubarb, berries like blackberries and blackcurrants and stone fruits like plums and apricots. They're a good thing to make if you find cheap, under-ripe fruit. Bramley apples are the best to use for cooking. They have a great flavour and go fabulously fluffy.

2 large Bramley apples
125g blackberries, picked wild or bought in season (late summer) or 125g mixed-frozen fruits
About 3 tbsp caster sugar (preferably unrefined)

Quarter, peel, core and slice the apples into a saucepan. Tip in the berries and add 3 tablespoons of sugar and 2 tablespoons of water. Put a lid on the pan and heat over a moderate heat until the fruit softens and collapses (about 10–15 minutes), stirring it occasionally. Pull the pan off the heat and check for sweetness, adding more sugar if you think it needs it. Give it a vigorous stir if you want a purée, rather than chunky fruit. Cool and refrigerate. To make your own fruit yoghurt, mix a good tablespoon of the compote with 2–3 tablespoons of plain yoghurt.

TRY THIS TOO...
• Also good reheated and served with hot custard if you have an open carton around from making the Banana Custard Yoghurt, opposite.

BANANA CUSTARD YOGHURT 🍁 Serves 1

Total comfort food. Mix ready-made custard (cheaper by the carton) with an equal quantity of plain yoghurt to make your own custard yoghurt.

1 small or ½ a medium ripe banana
1–2 tsp caster sugar, preferably unrefined
2 tbsp ready-to-serve custard
2 tbsp plain yoghurt
1 tbsp double or whipping cream, if you're feeling particularly indulgent

Peel and slice the banana into a bowl. Sprinkle over the sugar and mash it with a fork until completely smooth. Add the custard, yoghurt and cream, if using, and stir. (This mix also tastes fab semi-frozen. Simply add 3 tablespoons of milk, stir well and pop it in the freezer. Take it out after about an hour, stir well, sprinkle over a bit of chocolate flake or grated chocolate and eat).

TRY THIS TOO...

You could also make your own custard yoghurt with cooked rhubarb or mango pulp.

MANGO AND LIME SMOOTHIE 🍁 Serves 1–2

You occasionally find mangoes really cheap in markets. If you've got a blender they make fantastic smoothies.

1 small ripe mango
150ml–225ml plain yoghurt
1 tbsp lime or lemon juice

Hold the mango upright and cut vertically down each side, as near as you can get to the stone. Peel the slices you've made, then cut away the rest of the flesh from around the stone. Place the flesh and juice in a blender with 2 tablespoons of the yoghurt and whiz until smooth. Add the lime or lemon juice and half the remaining yoghurt and whiz again. Taste: if it's too mangoey add a bit more yoghurt, or too sweet, then add more lime. If it's just right, dilute to a drinkable consistency with a little water. Stir and serve.

RASPBERRY ROUGHIE 🍁 Serves 1

Roughies were a recipe I invented for the first Beyond Baked Beans *book to get around the problem of fancying a smoothie but not having a blender. I think raspberries make one of the best. They can be expensive out of season but are available frozen year round. Ripe strawberries also work well.*

75g (½ a small carton) fresh, or thawed frozen raspberries
½–1 tsp caster sugar
2 tbsp plain, low-fat yoghurt
Some muesli or crunchy cereal (optional)

Put the raspberries in a bowl and mash with the sugar. Stir in the yoghurt. Top with some muesli or crunchy cereal if you have some around.

Why does fruit taste so much better when it's cut up? (Discuss.) Supermarkets realise this, which is why they charge so much for pre-prepared fruit salads. But it's easy (and cheaper) to make them yourself, using whatever fruit is cheap and in season. (Don't overlook tinned fruit, but mix it with fresh fruit.) I like colour theming them, which is very sad and Martha Stewart-ish but it somehow looks more appealing and sophisticated. Or that's what I like to think anyway....

GREEN AND WHITE FRUIT SALAD ♥
Enough for 2 helpings

All you really need to make a fruit salad is two or three types of fruit. Choose as many as you like from the list below, or all, if you're feeling flush, in which case you could use fruit juice rather than having sugar syrup.

1 Granny Smith apple
1 tsp lemon juice
1 ripe pear or a wedge of honeydew melon
1 kiwi fruit
A few green grapes
100ml sugar syrup (see below) or apple juice

Wash the apple, quarter and core it and cut into small pieces. Put in a bowl and immediately mix in the lemon juice to stop it going brown. Quarter, peel and cut up the pear, or cut the melon off its rind and cut into cubes. Peel the kiwi fruit and cut into slices. Halve the grapes and remove the pips if they're not seedless. Mix all the fruit with sugar syrup or apple juice and serve. Leftovers should keep for 24 hours without the quality of the fruit spoiling.

TO MAKE SUGAR SYRUP
Put equal quantities of sugar (preferably unrefined caster sugar) and water in a saucepan (say, 225ml or a mug of each) and leave over a very low heat until all the grains have dissolved. Bring to the boil and boil for about 3–4 minutes. Cool before using. (You can also use this syrup for making cocktails.)

ORANGE AND YELLOW FRUIT SALAD ♥
Enough for 2 helpings

Exactly the same method but using as many of the following as you fancy or can afford.

1 small orange, clementine or mandarin, peeled and sliced or 1/2 a tin of mandarin oranges
A ripe peach or nectarine, or a few chunks of fresh or tinned mango or papaya, cut into cubes or 4 fresh or tinned apricot halves
Some fresh or tinned pineapple, skin removed and cut into small wedges
100ml sugar syrup or orange or tropical fruit juice

Remove pith from the orange by scoring with a sharp knife around the outside of the fruit as if you were cutting it into quarters (but cut only through the peel). Put in a bowl and pour over boiling water. Leave for a couple of minutes then drain off the water. The peel should come away easily, taking the pith with it. Cut the orange into slices like you would a tomato rather than breaking it into segments, cutting the larger slices into halves or quarters (looks better and you get more juice). If you have the cash you could buy a bottle of orange flower water to flavour your syrup with (use sparingly – a little goes a long way).

RED, BLACK AND BLUE FRUIT SALAD ❧
Enough for 2 helpings

More expensive than the others so only affordable in summer when soft fruits are cheap. Choose two or three of the following and follow the master recipe. (This one doesn't keep so well, so be sure to eat the same day.)

A few ripe strawberries, hulled (stalks removed) and sprinkled with sugar
A handful of raspberries
A few cherries – if you can be bothered to remove the stones – or a handful of blueberries or blackberries
Some black or red grapes
A splash of sugar syrup, pomegranate or grape juice – you don't need as much juice as with the other salads; the strawberries make some of their own juice.

£ WHAT TO DO WITH THE REST OF THE FRUIT

- **Apples** Good with Cheddar, or in salads (see p61).
- **Pears** Make a good salad with blue cheese, walnuts and a few salad leaves. Also fab with ice cream and chocolate sauce (see p137).
- **Grapes** Nice to nibble with brie.
- **Kiwi fruit** Dice and sprinkle them over muesli with yoghurt.
- **Honeydew melon** Good with ham. Also makes a surprisingly good savoury salad mixed with equal quantities of chopped tomato and cucumber and a light salad dressing (see p61). Add a little chopped mint if you have some.
- **Oranges** Squeeze them for fresh juice (good added to a carrot salad) or mix with apple, celery and walnuts and a tablespoon each of mayo and plain yoghurt for a Waldorf salad.
- **Peaches or nectarines** Great with soft creamy cheeses.
- **Mango** Make a Mango (or papaya) and Lime Smoothie (p79), or simply marinate in lime juice (p134).
- **Apricots** Make good spicy sauces – see the South African-Style Pork Chop on p54.
- **Pineapple** Add to salads – it goes well with sweetcorn, celery, peppers and ham for example. You could also add it to a stir-fry – see Sweet and Sour Chicken p58.
- **Strawberries and raspberries** Make a roughie (see p79).
- **Cherries and grapes** Great with brie.
- **Blueberries** Add to muesli or porridge (see p83).
- **Blackberries** Make a Blackberry and Apple Compote (see p78).

Porridge – as any self-respecting Scot will tell you – is a question of personal taste. Arguments rage over whether you should use milk or water, how thick you should make it and whether you should season it with sugar or salt. (Water, thick and salty is the traditional way!) Most Scots would be appalled at adding fruit which is what I like to do to it but it makes what is already a brilliantly healthy start to the day even healthier. (Oats are also a great source of slow release energy.) If you're going to make porridge regularly I suggest you buy some soft brown sugar, it makes it even tastier.

APPLE AND CINNAMON PORRIDGE 🍁 Serves 1

3 tbsp porridge oats (25–30g)
100ml semi-skimmed milk
1 eating apple or ½ a Bramley apple peeled and cut into small pieces
A small handful of raisins (optional but good)
About 1 tbsp soft brown sugar, demerara sugar or ordinary sugar
A small pinch (about ¼ tsp) cinnamon

Rinse a small, preferably non-stick pan with cold water (makes it easier to clean afterwards!). Put the oats, milk, 100ml (just under ½ a mug) water, chopped apple, raisins, sugar and cinnamon in the pan and bring slowly to the boil, stirring occasionally. Turn the heat down and simmer for 3–4 minutes. Serve with a little extra milk and sugar to taste. (Put the pan to soak as soon as you've poured out your porridge.)

BANANA AND HONEY PORRIDGE 🍁 Serves 1

1 small, ripe banana, sliced
3 tbsp porridge oats (25–30g)
200ml semi-skimmed milk
1 dessertspoon (2 tsp) clear honey or about 1 tbsp soft brown sugar, demerara sugar or ordinary sugar

Peel and slice the banana and put it in a small non-stick saucepan with the oats, milk and honey and cook as above. A spoonful of double cream is particularly yummy stirred in at the end. You could also add a few chopped nuts if you have some. Almonds would be specially good.

BLACK FOREST PORRIDGE ❦ Serves 1

This is based on those frozen fruit mixes that are incomprehensibly called black forest fruit mix or fruits of the forest. They generally contain blackberries, blackcurrants, blueberries and cherries and can be quite tart – hence the need for extra sugar. If the resulting purple colour of the porridge doesn't appeal, you could cook the berries separately and stir them into the finished porridge, but that does mean two pans.

3 tbsp porridge oats (25–30g)
200ml semi-skimmed milk
100g frozen or fresh mixed berries (see above)
2–3 tbsp soft brown, demerara or ordinary sugar
Low-fat fromage frais or yoghurt to serve

Put the oats, milk, berries and sugar in a small pan then follow the method in the apple and cinnamon porridge recipe (see opposite). Stir in some low-fat fromage frais or yoghurt to serve.

BASIC MUESLI WITH APPPLE AND RAISINS ❦ Serves 1

You can use porridge oats to make a simple muesli too.

3 tbsp porridge oats
100ml apple juice or milk
A handful of raisins
A few chopped nuts if you have some
1 tsp soft brown sugar
1/2 a crisp apple, cored and peeled
Plain or soy yoghurt to serve

Spoon the oats into a cereal bowl. Pour over the apple juice or milk, stir in the raisins, and nuts if you have some, add the sugar and leave for 5 minutes. Grate the apple into the bowl, adding a little more liquid if you think it needs it. Serve with yoghurt.

TRY THIS TOO...

You could use raspberries or blueberries rather than raisins if you find some reduced.

There are certain ingredients that lend themselves so well to leftovers. It's worth deliberately making more than you need so that you can heat them up the next day. Here's to potatoes, rice and couscous.

POTATOES

The best way to use up leftover potatoes is to make a hash. New potatoes work best but are more expensive. If you're cooking old potatoes for mash take a few out before they're quite ready, so they don't disintegrate. You can simply fry them up with a few onions or spice them up rather more sexily.

SAMOSA HASH ♨
Serves 1

More or less the filling you put in a samosa.

2 tbsp vegetable oil
1 medium onion, peeled and roughly chopped
1 clove of garlic, peeled and crushed or finely chopped
1 small green chilli, de-seeded and finely chopped (optional)
1/2 tsp cumin seeds (optional)
1/2 tsp mild curry paste or powder plus 1/4 tsp turmeric if you have some
4 or 5 cooked new potatoes or about 2 cooked old potatoes, cut into cubes
A handful of frozen peas, thawed
2 tbsp fresh coriander
Salt

Heat the oil in a frying pan. Add the onion and fry over a moderate heat for about 5 minutes until beginning to brown. Turn the heat down and stir in the garlic and chilli and cumin seeds, if using, then add the curry paste or powder and turmeric. Cook for a minute, add the potato and peas and turn them over in the spices. Cook for another 2–3 minutes until the vegetables have heated through and then take off the heat. Stir in the fresh coriander and season to taste with salt. Good – hot or cold – with wholewheat pitta bread.

CORNED BEEF HASH
Serves 1

The classic American hash.

2 tbsp vegetable oil
1 medium onion, peeled and
   roughly chopped
$1/2$ a green or red, pepper,
   de-seeded and roughly
   chopped (optional)
1 clove of garlic, peeled and
   crushed or finely chopped
$1/2$–1 tsp mild chilli powder or
   $1/2$ tsp paprika
$1/3$ to $1/2$ a 340g tin of corned
   beef, cut into cubes
2–3 cooked potatoes, cut into
   cubes
1 tbsp chopped fresh parsley
   (optional)
Salt and ground black pepper

Heat the oil in a large frying pan or wok. Cook the onion over a moderate heat until beginning to brown (about 5–6 minutes). Add the garlic and chilli powder and cook for another minute then add the corned beef and potatoes. Fry the mixture, turning it over occasionally until it begins to accumulate some nice crusty bits (about 5–6 minutes). Add the chopped parsley, if using, and season with salt and pepper. Serve with ketchup or hot pepper sauce.

£ LEFTOVER CORN BEEF?

Cut thick slices and make a fry-up with fried egg and tomatoes. Or use them in sandwiches with tomatoes and sliced sweet and sour cucumbers or piccalilli.

EASY POTATO SALAD

Two things to remember about potato salad: use new potatoes rather than old ones and don't let them get cold before you make the salad.

$1/4$ tsp mustard (optional but
   it does make a difference)
2 tsp wine vinegar
$2 1/2$ tbsp sunflower or olive oil
3 or 4 freshly cooked, warm
   new potatoes
2 spring onions, trimmed and
   finely sliced, or a couple of
   finely chopped slices of onion
Salt and ground black pepper

Put the mustard, vinegar and a little salt and pepper into a bowl and whisk together with a fork. Gradually add the oil till you have a thick dressing. Slice the potatoes into the dressing, add the onion and toss together. Good with cold ham or hot frankfurters.

RICE

It really is worth making enough rice for at least two meals. Choose Basmati which has by far the best flavour and doesn't cost a fortune considering how little you need for a helping (50–75g, depending on your appetite).

PERFECT FLUFFY RICE
Serves 1 + enough for another meal

Tip 100–150g of Basmati rice into a saucepan of boiling, salted water, stir once then boil for 10 minutes. Drain in a colander or sieve, then balance the sieve over the saucepan and cover it with a piece of kitchen towel. After 5 minutes, pour away any water that has accumulated in the pan, tip in the rice and fork it through to fluff it up. To use later in egg-fried rice or a quick pilau, spoon out half into a bowl, cool, cover and refrigerate it.

EGG-FRIED RICE ✿
Serves 1

1 large or 2 medium eggs, preferably free-range
2 tbsp sunflower or vegetable oil
2–3 spring onions trimmed and finely sliced or 1 small onion peeled and finely chopped
A portion of cooked basmati rice (see above)
50g frozen peas, cooked or thawed
About 1 tbsp light soy sauce

Break the eggs into a bowl and beat them lightly. Heat a wok or large frying pan over a moderate heat and pour in the oil.
Tip in the onions and stir-fry for 2–3 minutes until beginning to soften. Add the eggs and stir until almost all the liquid egg has disappeared (a few seconds). Add the rice and peas and stir-fry for a couple of minutes until hot through. Sprinkle over soy sauce to taste.

£ BULK IT OUT
To make this more substantial you could add sliced button mushrooms.

QUICK SPICED RICE
INDIAN STYLE

Just stir-fry an onion for 2–3 minutes until beginning to soften. Stir in a crushed clove of garlic and 1/2 teaspoons of curry powder or paste. Add some chopped leftover chicken or a handful of frozen prawns and fry over a moderate heat for 2–3 minutes. Tip in the rice and a few frozen peas and stir-fry for another 2 minutes until hot through. Season with salt and a squeeze of lemon. Stir in some fresh coriander if you have some.

SPANISH STYLE

Add half a pepper, de-seeded and cubed and some chopped bacon or – even better – some chorizo, or other spicy sausage, to the onion as you fry it. Stir in a small clove of crushed or finely chopped garlic, 1/4–1/2 teaspoons of paprika and 1/4 teaspoon of turmeric. Then tip in the rice and peas and heat through as above. Stir in some parsley.

COUSCOUS

Couscous is actually simpler to cook than potatoes, pasta or rice. You simply pour over hot water (or, better still, veggie stock), add a little oil, let it absorb the liquid then fluff it up with a fork. On its own it makes a good accompaniment to spicy bean and vegetable stews. Any leftovers can be used for a salad like this one.

COURGETTE AND PRAWN COUSCOUS SALAD

A portion of cooked couscous (about 125g cooked weight – or make up some following the instructions below)
2 tbsp sunflower oil or light olive oil
2–3 spring onions, trimmed and finely sliced
1 medium courgette, trimmed and coarsely grated
75g ready-to-eat frozen prawns
Salt and lemon juice to taste
1 heaped tbsp finely chopped fresh parsley, mint or coriander

If you haven't got any leftover couscous, make up about 60ml (about 4 tablespoons) following the instructions on the pack, but substituting vegetable stock for water. Heat a frying pan, add the oil, heat for a few seconds then chuck in the spring onions and grated courgette and fry over a high heat for about 2 minutes. Tip the vegetables into the cooked couscous along with the prawns and fork through. Season to taste with salt, pepper and a good squeeze of lemon. Stir in some chopped herbs – whatever you've got to hand.

TRY THIS TOO...
You can also make a good couscous salad with leftover roast onions, roast peppers (see p64) and/or roast butternut squash and some white crumbly cheese.

SHARE

You don't need to be studying for a maths degree to realise that if you pool your resources you'll have a bigger household budget to play with. That isn't of course always practicable but you could at least have a couple of meals with housemates or friends each week to spread the load.

Quite apart from anything else, eating should be sociable – sitting down together is a more relaxing way to eat than shovelling down a meal in front of the telly. It also justifies switching on the oven – which brings recipes like roasts and bakes into play. And it's actually easier to make one-pot dishes and chunky soups to feed a crowd than to make them for one, particularly if you can persuade one of your mates to act as sous chef and do all the chopping.

You can also, of course, use many of the dishes in 'Survive'. Just double or treble the quantities as necessary. But don't count on having any leftovers....

Probably everyone's favourite roast, almost always on special offer, chicken is the perfect answer to that traditional Sunday lunch.

LEMON ROAST CHICKEN
Serves 4 (or 1 + leftovers – see pp48–53)

Even cheap chicken can be made really tasty – the key is the long, slow cooking.

1 medium-sized chicken
  (about 1.5kg)
1 fresh lemon
2 cloves of garlic
Vegetable or sunflower oil
Salt and black pepper

Preheat the oven to 200C/400F/ Gas 6. Remove any giblets from the chicken and pat it dry with kitchen towel. Cut the lemon in half and squeeze the juice of one half over the chicken, rubbing it in well, then put the squeezed half of the lemon and 2 smashed cloves of garlic inside the bird. Smother the chicken with oil and pour a little oil in a roasting tin. Season the chicken with salt and pepper and put it breast side upwards in the tin. Roast for 20 minutes then turn the heat down to 190C/ 375F/Gas 5 and cook for another $1^1/_4$ hours, occasionally spooning over the juices in the tin. Cover the breast with foil if it's getting too brown. About 20 minutes before the end of the cooking time carefully tilt the pan and pour the excess fat into a bowl. Squeeze the remaining lemon over the breast and put the squeezed half in the tin.

Pour in a small glass of water and return the bird to the oven. When the chicken has cooked remove it from the tin and place it on a large plate or clean chopping board. Cover lightly with foil and leave to rest for 10–15 minutes while you make the gravy. Spoon off any remaining visible fat then pour in another small glass of water and work it around the base of the tin with a wooden spoon to loosen any stuck on cooking juices. Bubble the gravy up and season to taste – it should be nice and lemony. Serve with roast potatoes (see opposite) or new potatoes and peas.

REALLY GOOD ROAST POTATOES 🍁 Serves 4

The packaging or labels on potatoes indicate whether they're suitable for roasting. Basically you want old potatoes for this method. The way to get them really crunchy is to boil them for a short while before you roast them and then give them a fierce blast of heat at the end.

1.25 kg old potatoes
About 5–6 tbsp vegetable oil

Preheat the oven to 200 C/400F/Gas 6. (This is the ideal temperature to cook roast potatoes but if you're cooking a chicken at a lower temperature just give them a bit longer.) Peel the potatoes, halve or quarter them depending how big they are and place them in a large saucepan. Cover with cold water and bring to the boil. Add a little salt, boil for 5 minutes then strain off the water. Pour a thin layer of oil into a roasting tin and tip in the potatoes, turning them in the oil. Roast the potatoes for 45 minutes turning them half way through. Turn the heat up to 220 C/425 F/Gas 7 and continue to cook until the potatoes are crisp (about another 15 minutes).

ROAST NEW POTATOES WITH GARLIC 🍁

If you're roasting new potatoes you don't need to pre-boil them or blast them at the end. Just cut them up small and tip them into the oil as described above. Roast them at 190C–200C/375F–400F/Gas 5–6 (whichever temperature you've got your oven on) for about an hour. When you turn them, add 5–6 unpeeled cloves of garlic, shaking the pan so they get coated in oil. If you've got some fresh rosemary chuck a few sprigs of that in too. (As this is easier than the above recipe you might wonder why I don't suggest this as the main roast potato recipe. Because new potatoes are more expensive and most people prefer them crustier, that's why!)

CHEAT'S ROAST CHICKEN WITH BACON, CRISPS AND ONION PORRIDGE
Serves 4

This is exactly the same as roasting a whole bird other than the fact that you don't have to carve it. Serving crisps, as is traditional with game birds, saves you having to bother roasting potatoes. And the onion porridge? A cheap, surprisingly tasty replacement for bread sauce.

2 tbsp vegetable oil or other cooking oil
1kg chicken thighs and drumsticks or chicken legs, free-range if possible
1/2 tsp dried thyme (optional)
8 streaky bacon rashers
4 cloves of garlic (optional)
Salt and pepper
A large packet of salted (rather than flavoured) crisps

Preheat the oven to 200 C/400F/Gas 6. Spoon the oil into a roasting tin then put in the chicken pieces. Turn them in the oil and season with salt, pepper and a little thyme, if you have some. Put the tin in the oven and cook the chicken for 30 minutes. Start cooking the onion porridge, if you're making it. Cut the rind off the bacon rashers, if necessary and then stretch each rasher by running the blunt edge of the knife along the rasher. When 30 minutes is up, take out the tin from the oven and turn over the chicken pieces. Season them on the other side. Tuck the garlic cloves, if using, between the chicken pieces and arrange the bacon rashers over the top. Replace the tin in the oven. After another 15 minutes turn the heat up to 220C/425F/ Gas 7 and continue to cook until the bacon is crisp (another 10–15 minutes). In the meantime, make the gravy (see opposite). Serve with the crisps and either peas or sprouts (or both!).

ONION PORRIDGE
Serves 4

Homage to one of Britain's most celebrated chefs Heston Blumenthal, who revived the idea of savoury porridge by putting it on the menu of his 3 Michelin-starred restaurant, The Fat Duck. It works surprisingly well – try it!

A good slice (25g) butter
1 medium onion, peeled and roughly chopped
1 clove of garlic, peeled and crushed
50g porridge oats
175ml light vegetable stock made with 1 tsp vegetable bouillon powder
175ml whole or semi-skimmed milk
2–3 tbsp finely chopped parsley (optional but good)
Salt, ground black pepper and lemon juice to taste

Heat the butter gently in a small saucepan, add the onion and garlic and stir. Put a lid on the pan and cook over a very low heat for 10–15 minutes, until it's completely soft but not brown. Stir in the porridge oats, vegetable stock and milk, bring to the boil and simmer for about 3–4 minutes, adding the parsley, if using. Season to taste with salt, pepper and a small squeeze of lemon juice. Serve hot. It's good, not only with chicken, but sausages too.

AMAZING MARMITE GRAVY 🍁 Serves 4

Although there are now some quite reasonable ready-made stocks around they're not cheap, so I'd still stick to this foolproof recipe that first appeared in Beyond Baked Beans. *Much, much better than gravy granules and no, it doesn't really taste of Marmite.*

25g butter
1½ tbsp plain flour
1½–2 tsp Marmite

Measure out 400ml of boiling water and stir in the Marmite until it dissolves. Melt the butter gently in a saucepan and stir in the flour. Cook over a low heat for a minute then add the Marmite stock, stirring continuously. Bring back to the boil and simmer until thick. Check to see if it's meaty enough. If not, spoon off a couple of tablespoons of the gravy, mix in a little extra Marmite and return it to the pan. (Note the absence of seasoning. Marmite is quite salty enough and oddly it doesn't seem to need pepper.)

UNSOGGY SPROUTS

Sprouts go curiously well with chicken – and turkey of course. If you haven't bought them ready-trimmed (remember, you're saving money!), here's how to prepare and cook them.

500g sprouts
A good slice of butter
Salt and pepper

Take a thin slice off the end of the stalk and remove any damaged outside leaves. If the sprouts are large, cut a cross in the base to help them cook. Put them in a saucepan, cover with boiling water, bring back to the boil and cook for 7–10 minutes, depending on size. Check how they're doing by inserting a sharp knife in one. It should slide in without any resistance. Drain, add the butter and season with salt and pepper.

Minced beef isn't the bargain it once was, particularly the 'extra lean' type that can be quite pricey. If you're keeping the cost down the answer is to use less, or use another type of meat like pork or turkey – both good options.

BUDGET BOLOGNESE 1
Serves 4

Apart from the Marmite this is a reasonably authentic Italian recipe – a modest quantity of meat, bulked out by a generous amount of veggies. The only downside is that it takes a long time to cook – but you can leave it simmering away just like a stew.

4 tbsp olive, sunflower or
   vegetable oil
250–300g minced beef
2–3 slices back or streaky
   bacon (about 75g), rind
   removed and very finely
   chopped (optional)
1 medium onion (about 125g),
   peeled and very finely
   chopped
1 clove of garlic, peeled and
   very finely chopped
1 medium carrot (about 75g),
   peeled and very finely
   chopped
1 stick of celery, very finely
   chopped (optional)
2 tbsp wine vinegar
1½ tbsp tomato paste
1 x 400g tin whole tomatoes
150ml stock made with ½ tsp
   Marmite (p93)
Salt and black pepper
400g spaghetti
Parmesan or Cheddar cheese
   to serve

Heat a saucepan or casserole for 2–3 minutes until hot, add 1 tablespoon of the oil and fry the beef until lightly browned on all sides. Scoop the beef out of the pan with a large spoon, leaving the fat behind then discard the fat (see opposite). Add 3 more tablespoons of oil, heat through for a minute then add the bacon. Fry for a minute, then add the onion, stir and cook for 3–4 minutes over a low heat until the onion starts to soften.

Add the garlic, chopped carrot and celery, cover the pan and fry for another 5–6 minutes. Return the meat to the pan, fry for a couple of minutes then pour in the wine vinegar and bubble up for a minute or two until evaporated. Stir in the tomato paste and mix well with the meat and vegetables. Add the tinned tomatoes and break down with a wooden spoon. Pour in the stock, stir and bring to the boil. Turn the heat right down, partially cover the pan and leave the sauce to simmer for 1½–2 hours, stirring the sauce occasionally. About 15 minutes before you want to eat put the spaghetti on to cook in a large pan of boiling, salted water, following the instructions on the pack (see p36).
Spoon a little cooking water into the sauce. Drain the spaghetti. Check the seasoning for the sauce, adding salt and pepper if necessary. Divide the spaghetti between 4 plates, spoon the sauce on top and grate over a little Parmesan or Cheddar.

BUDGET BOLOGNESE 2
Serves 4

An alternative bolognese – lighter and creamier – based on turkey or pork mince both of which tend to be cheaper than beef mince.

2–3 tbsp vegetable oil
450g pork or turkey mince
A thin slice of butter (about 10–12g)
250g mushrooms, rinsed and very finely chopped
2 tbsp tomato paste
2 cloves of garlic, peeled and crushed
1/2 a 400g tin whole or chopped tomatoes or 150ml creamed tomatoes or passata
Just over 100ml stock made with boiling water and 1/2 tsp Marmite
400g spaghetti
A small carton of whipping cream or double cream
Salt, pepper and lemon juice or wine vinegar to taste
2–3 tbsp finely chopped parsley if you have some

Heat a frying pan and add 1 tablespoon of vegetable oil. Once the oil is hot, fry the mince until browned then remove it from the pan with a large spoon letting the fat drain away. Pour off the fat into a bowl. Add the remaining oil to the pan then add the butter. Tip in the mushrooms and stir-fry over a high heat for about 3–4 minutes until any moisture has evaporated. Turn the heat down and return the mince to the pan. Add the tomato paste and garlic and cook for a minute then add the tomatoes or passata. (If using whole tomatoes break them down with a wooden spoon or a fork.) Add the stock, stir and leave the sauce simmering over a low heat while you cook the spaghetti (see p36). Once the spaghetti has drained add about two thirds of the cream to the sauce and heat through gently. Season the sauce with salt, pepper and a few drops of lemon juice or wine vinegar. Stir in some chopped parsley if you have some. I don't think this needs cheese but feel free if you fancy it.

DON'T BLOCK THE SINK!
Don't pour fat down the sink – it may block it! It's better to pour it into a cup or bowl, let it solidify then wrap and dispose of it.)

Mince always seems to taste more appealing if it's combined with sausage meat and made into a meatloaf or meatballs. You can vary them endlessly depending on what type of mince (beef, lamb, pork or turkey) and what kind of sausage you use.

EASY MEATLOAF
Serves 6

This uses porridge oats rather than the traditional breadcrumbs. It may sound weird but don't worry. Once the meatloaf is cooked you won't taste them but they help to make the meatloaf go further.

400–450g decent sausages e.g. Cumberland
400–450g minced beef
3 rashers of lean back bacon (about 90–100g)
2 cloves of garlic, peeled and crushed
1/2 a bunch of spring onions, trimmed and finely sliced or a small onion, peeled and finely chopped
3 heaped tbsp chopped parsley or 1 1/2 tsp dried Herbes de Provence
50g porridge oats
1 large egg, lightly beaten plus enough semi-skimmed milk to make 175ml of liquid
Ground black pepper
You'll need a 900g loaf tin or ovenproof dish, lightly oiled

Preheat the oven to 180C/350F/ Gas 4. Cut the links between the sausages. Cut through the skin of each sausage and pull it off. Put the sausage meat into a large bowl with the mince. Add the crushed garlic, spring onions and parsley and mix together well with a fork, wooden spoon or your hands. Sprinkle over the porridge oats, pour over the egg and milk mixture and mix together thoroughly. Sprinkle generously with pepper and mix again. Pack the mixture into a lightly oiled large loaf tin or an ovenware dish. Place the dish in a roasting tin and pour boiling water around it up to the depth of about 1.5cm. Bake for about an hour or until the meatloaf has shrunk well away from the sides of the tin. Carefully pour off any fat that has accumulated then tip the meatloaf onto a serving plate. Turn it upright and slice it thickly. Serve with double the quantity of Winter or Summer Napoli Sauce (pp36-37) or gravy (p93). Plain boiled potatoes and lightly cooked, buttered cabbage go well with this.

£ KEEP IT CHEAP
Sausages are generally cheaper than sausage meat – see p16 for sausage buying tips.

£ LEFTOVERS?
Great cold with pickles.

EASY MEATBALLS
Serves 4–6

The same idea as the meatloaf, just tweaking the ingredients and forming the mixture into balls. You can make them without the breadcrumbs and beaten egg but they make the mixture slightly easier to handle – and stretch further.

400–450g decent sausages, skinned (as described above)

400g–500g minced beef
4 cloves of garlic, peeled and crushed
3 heaped tbsp finely chopped fresh parsley plus extra for sauce
3 tbsp dried natural breadcrumbs (not the horrid bright orange ones)
1 medium egg, lightly beaten
Plain flour for rolling the meatballs
5–6 tbsp sunflower or vegetable oil
2 x 400g tins of tomatoes
Salt and ground black pepper
A little sugar for seasoning
Grated Parmesan (optional)

Mix all the ingredients apart from the flour, oil, tomatoes and sugar as described for Easy Meatloaf. Sprinkle a chopping board with flour. Scoop out heaped teaspoons of the mix (or a dessertspoon, if you want a bigger meatball), dip them in the flour and roll them between your palms. Heat 3 tablespoons of the oil in a large frying pan or wok and fry the meatballs in batches browning them on all sides. Set aside on a plate. When you've

fried all the meatballs pour away any excess fat and rinse and dry the pan. Pour in the remaining oil, heat for a minute then add the remaining garlic and fry for a few seconds. Tip in the tomatoes and break them down with a fork or wooden spoon. Cook over a moderately high heat for 5 minutes until jammy and season to taste with salt, pepper and a little sugar. Tip in the meatballs, and turn them over in the sauce, ensuring they're well covered. Cover the pan and cook the meatballs over a low heat for about half an hour, spooning over the sauce occasionally and adding a little extra water if it's becoming too dry. After 15 minutes cook some spaghetti or rice to go with the meatballs (see p36 and 86). To serve, stir in some more parsley and spoon the meatballs and sauce over the spaghetti or rice. Sprinkle with grated Parmesan if you have some.

A SPICY TWIST

If you want to spice up the recipe use spicy sausages or

add a teaspoon of paprika to the meat mix. You could also add 8–10 finely chopped green olives if the budget will run to them. Add $1/2$ a teaspoon of paprika to the tomato sauce too. You could serve this with chickpeas.

A MIDDLE-EASTERN FLAVOUR

Mix the sausage meat with lamb mince (or beef mince with lamb sausages, whichever is cheapest). Season with 1 tablespoon of Moroccan Spice Mix (p19) and replace some or all of the parsley with chopped fresh coriander and a little chopped mint if you have some. Serve with pitta bread and Tzatziki, doubling or trebling the quantity on p60).

EASY BURGERS
Makes 8 burgers

Follow the meatball recipe but shape into round patties. Flour and fry them in oil over a moderate heat for about 3 minutes a side. Serve with salad.

SAUSAGE AND MASH WITH ONION GRAVY
Serves 4

Having written a book titled Sausage and Mash. *I feel I could do a PhD on the subject. Here's a good simple version. Personally I prefer frying them, but shoving them in the oven is undoubtedly less messy and leaves you more room on the top of the stove. I've given both options.*

2 x packs of decent quality
   sausages e.g. Cumberland
   (see p16)
3 tbsp oil
For the mash
4–5 large potatoes, about 900g
   in total
A good slice of butter (about
   40g)
50–75ml warm milk
Sea salt and freshly ground
   black pepper

If you're baking the sausages heat the oven to 200C/400F /Gas 6. While it's heating peel the potatoes and halve or quarter them so you have even-sized pieces. Place them in a saucepan, cover with cold water and bring to the boil (about 5 minutes). Skim off any froth, season them with salt then cook for 20–25 minutes until you can put the tip of a knife into them without any resistance. Meanwhile put 2 tablespoons of the oil in a roasting tin and heat it in the oven for about 4–5 minutes. Cut the links between the sausages and tip them into the pan, turning them so they are evenly covered with oil. Return to the oven and cook for about 20 minutes, turning them occasionally. If you're frying the sausage, heat the oil in a pan over a moderate heat, add the sausages, turn the heat down slightly and cook for 20 minutes, turning occasionally. Pour off any excess fat if they seem to be stewing rather than frying. While the sausages and spuds are cooking make the gravy (see opposite). Once the potatoes are cooked pour off the water (or drain them in a colander and return them to the pan). Put the pan of potatoes back over the heat for a few seconds to dry up any excess moisture. Take the pan off the heat, chop the potatoes up roughly with a knife then mash them with a potato masher or a fork until they are smooth and lump free. Beat in the butter and enough warm milk to make a soft but not sloppy consistency. Season with salt and black pepper. Once cooked they'll keep warm for about 20 minutes with the pan lid on. Serve the sausages with a good dollop of mash and gravy spooned over.

£ TRY THIS TOO...
Root veg like swedes, carrots and parsnips also make good mash, though they are harder to get smooth unless you have a hand-held blender or food processor.

FOR THE ONION GRAVY
Serves 4

3 medium onions (about 300–350g), peeled and sliced
1 tbsp cooking oil
A lump of butter (about 20g)
1 tbsp plain flour
350ml of stock made with boiling water and 1½ tsp Marmite
Black pepper
Soy sauce or brown sauce to taste (optional)

Heat a heavy saucepan or small frying pan over a moderate heat, add the oil then a few seconds later, the butter. Tip in the onions, stir well and cook over a medium heat for 10–15 minutes until soft and beginning to brown. Stir in the flour and gradually add the hot stock, stirring well as you go. Bring to the boil then turn the heat right down and simmer for 5 minutes, or until ready to use it. Season with pepper and a few drops of soy sauce or brown sauce if you have some.

BUBBLE & SQUEAK
Serves 4

A great way of using up leftover cooked potatoes and cabbage or sprouts, but can also be cooked from scratch. Goes well with any type of pork sausage.

About 500g each of cold boiled potatoes and cooked cabbage or sprouts
Salt and freshly ground black pepper
1 tbsp olive oil
25g butter

Roughly chop up the potato and cabbage, mix together and season well with salt and pepper. Heat a large frying pan over a moderate heat, add the oil, heat for a minute then add the butter. Tip in the potato and cabbage mix and flatten into a cake with a fork or a spatula. Let it cook for about 2-3 minutes then start to turn it over. Keep turning it every few minutes until the crispy bits on the bottom of the pan get well mixed in to the hash – about 8-10 minutes in all.

100 GORGEOUS GOULASH

PORK, PEPPER AND POTATO GOULASH
Serves 6–8

If you want to have several friends round and don't want too much last minute hassle this is the perfect all-in-one dish. It's also economical. I invented it for a Red Nose Day feast and it's been a firm favourite with my kids ever since.

1.5kg pork shoulder steaks
4 tbsp sunflower oil or other light cooking oil
500g onions, peeled and finely sliced
2 large cloves of garlic, peeled and finely chopped
3–4 tsp paprika or, better still, Spanish pimenton
1 tbsp tomato paste
2 level tbsp plain flour
1 tsp of dried oregano or Herbes de Provence
500ml passata
250ml light chicken or vegetable stock made with 1$\frac{1}{2}$ tsp vegetable bouillon powder
2 large or 3 medium red peppers
1kg new potatoes
Salt and ground black pepper

To serve
284ml carton of sour cream
6–8 sweet and sour pickled cucumbers, finely sliced (optional but good)

You will also need a large heavy saucepan or casserole

Trim the pork steaks of excess fat (but don't worry about leaving a bit – it will help the texture of the goulash) and cut into large cubes. Heat a large casserole or frying pan, add 1 tablespoon of the oil, heat through again then add enough pork pieces to cover the pan in a single layer. Brown on both sides, remove with a slotted spoon and set the meat aside. Continue browning the remaining meat, adding a little extra oil with each batch. Once you've fried all the meat add another 2 tablespoons of oil to the pan and tip in the onions. Stir and fry them for about 5–6 minutes until beginning to soften. Add the garlic, paprika and tomato paste, stir well then return the meat to the pan. Stir to ensure the meat is thoroughly coated and then add the flour, oregano or Herbes de Provence, passata and stock. Bring to the boil then cover the pan, turn the heat right down to a bare simmer or transfer the pot to a low oven (150 C/300 F/Gas 2). Cook for 2 hours, checking from time to time that the meat is not cooking too fast. After an hour, cut up, de-seed and slice the peppers, removing any white pith, add them to the pot, stir and replace the lid. Cut the potatoes into even-sized pieces and cook in boiling water for 10 minutes. Drain and add them to the pan half an hour before the end of the cooking time, carefully mixing them into the sauce. Check the seasoning, adding salt and pepper to taste. Stir the sour cream and spoon a little over each portion as you serve up. Offer the pickled cucumbers to go with.

TRY THIS TOO...

• If you don't eat pork just make this with beef. You may have to increase the cooking time slightly though.
• If you don't eat meat substitute 1kg of mushrooms for the pork.
• You can leave out the new potatoes and serve it with baked potatoes if you prefer.

PAPRIKA v PIMENTON: WHICH ONE?

Hungarians would of course disagree, but in my view the best paprika in the world is Spanish pimenton, it has a fabulous smoky flavour. You can buy it in two strengths: dulce (sweet) or piccante (spicy). A small tin should last a term at least unless you're using it every day (which is tempting). If you're going to buy only one: I'd choose the dulce which rounds out sauces without making them unduly hot. You can always ratchet up the heat with some chilli sauce or powder if you need to.

Those of you who have bought previous *Beyond Baked Beans* books will know that I don't regard baked potatoes as the great student panacea. It really only makes sense to cook them when you have enough people to justify turning on the oven. Then, I admit, they can make a cheap, substantial and filling meal, particularly if you exercise a bit of inventiveness over the toppings. The best time of year for baked potatoes is in the winter when potatoes are a good size but haven't been in cold store for an eternity. Choose ones that are labelled as suitable for baking.

NICE FLUFFY BAKED POTATOES
Serves 4–6

The mistake most people make when cooking baked potatoes is to buy absolutely gigantic ones that take an age to cook and end up like a soggy football. If you're cooking several at once they also need to be even-sized so you don't end up with a mix of over- and under-cooked potatoes.

4–6 large but not ridiculously large potatoes (about 250–300g each)
A little sunflower or vegetable oil

Preheat the oven to 200C/400F/ Gas 6. Give the potatoes a good scrub if dirty and dry well with kitchen towel. Prick the skin with a fork in several places to ensure the potatoes don't burst (not necessary if you have a spike – see below). Pour a little oil into your palms and rub it over the potatoes (this makes the skin nice and crisp). Put the potatoes on a baking tray or in a roasting tin for about an hour to an hour and a quarter, turning them half way through.
Cut a cross in the centre of each baked potato as you take it out of the oven then, protecting your hands with oven gloves, squeeze the sides of the potato so it opens up at the top.
This lets the steam escape and makes the potato fluffier.

HIGH SPEED POTATOES!
To speed up the cooking time impale the potatoes on a baked potato spike. You can buy them in department stores, kitchen shops or those weird catalogues of gadgets nobody really needs. Except potato spikes, obviously.

TRY THIS TOO...
You can also roast sweet potatoes the same way. They tend to be smaller so will take slightly less time – about 45–50 minutes. They go really well with chilli and spiced vegetable stews.

SOME GOOD TOPPINGS

COTTAGE CHEESE TZATZIKI

Made very much in the same way as conventional Tzatziki (p60). For 4–6, mix a 227g carton of cottage cheese, with a crushed clove of garlic, about a tablespoon of finely chopped onion or spring onion and 2 tablespoons of plain yoghurt. Peel and coarsely grate a third of a cucumber, squeeze out the excess moisture and add to the cottage cheese along with 5–6 finely chopped mint leaves or some chopped, fresh parsley. Season with salt and pepper.

PRAWNS AND MAYO

Mix 200g fresh or thawed, frozen prawns with 3 tablespoons of mayo mixed with 3 tablespoons of plain yoghurt. Add a little finely chopped spring onion or some snipped chives if you have some.

OR ANY OF THE FOLLOWING...

• Basic bolognese or chilli (pp42–43) or either of the bolognese sauces (pp94–95).
• All variations on baked beans (p66).
• Blue cheese, sour cream and bacon.
• Soft garlic and herb 'roulé' cheese (supermarket own brands are cheapest).
• Roast peppers (p64). These can be cooked at the same time as the potatoes and goats' cheese.

AND A GOOD STUFFING TOO

CHEESE, ONION & BACON STUFFED BAKED POTATOES

Life, you might think, is too short to stuff a potato but you get the best of all worlds – crispy baked potato skin, mashed potato filling and crispy cheesy crust. Mmmmm.

4 x medium to large potatoes, about 250g–300g each
3 tbsp vegetable or sunflower oil
1 medium onion, peeled and finely chopped
4 back bacon rashers or 8 streaky rashers (about 125g in total), finely chopped
A good slice (25g) butter
4–5 tbsp milk or a mixture of milk and cream, sour cream or fromage frais
125g mature Cheddar, grated

Preheat the oven to 200C/400F /Gas 6. Scrub the potatoes clean, dry them, prick them with a fork and rub them lightly with oil. Bake them for an hour to an hour and a quarter, turning them half way through. (You can go off and do something else at this point.) Take the potatoes out of the oven and leave to cool slightly while you heat the remaining oil and fry the chopped onion and bacon until crisp. Cut the potatoes in half and carefully scoop out the centre without breaking the skin. Mash until smooth then add the butter and milk or milk and cream and mash again. Add the fried onion and bacon and a third of the cheese, mix well together and season with salt and pepper. Pile the filling back into the potatoes, top with the remaining grated cheese. Turn the oven up to 220C/425F/Gas 7 and cook the potatoes until the topping is nice and crispy. Good with salad or lightly cooked broccoli or spring greens.

TRY THIS TOO...
You could replace the Cheddar with other hard cheeses such as Lancashire or Red Leicester, a crumbly blue cheese like Stilton or a soft herb and garlic-flavoured cheese.

Potato bakes make fabulously, comforting meals and are dead easy provided you're willing to do a bit of slicing.

PORK, POTATO AND APPLE BAKE Serves 4

Pork chops are one of the best supermarket bargains. Pork is cheap anyway and many people are funny about bones making chops even cheaper. Once you've prepared the dish you just leave it to cook – no fiddling. It couldn't be easier.

4 large pork chops (about 800g in total)
2 tbsp vegetable oil plus a little extra for greasing the baking dish
1 large onion (about 225g), peeled and thinly sliced
2 sticks of celery or half a bulb of fennel, trimmed and sliced (optional)
1 large Bramley apple (about 225g), peeled and thinly sliced
$1/2$ tsp dried thyme or Herbes de Provence
1 level tsp ground coriander (optional)
350ml chicken or vegetable stock made with $1/2$ a stock cube or 2 tsp vegetable bouillon powder
2 tbsp cider or wine vinegar
3 medium-large potatoes (about 450–500g), peeled and thinly sliced
Salt and pepper

Preheat the oven to 190C/375F/Gas 5. Pat the chops dry with kitchen towel and season with salt and pepper. Heat a large frying pan for a couple of minutes then add the oil. When the oil is hot, fry the chops for about 2–3 minutes each side until lightly browned. Remove from the pan and add the onion, celery and apple, stir and fry for about 3–4 minutes until beginning to soften. Add the thyme and coriander, if using, then poor in the stock and vinegar. Lightly grease a roasting tin and lay the potato slices across the bottom. Tip in about a third of the onion and apple mixture, lay the chops on top then pour over the remaining vegetables. Loosely cover the chops with foil and bake them for about 50–60 minutes, depending on how thick they are. Remove the foil for the last 10 minutes. Serve with a green salad or some lightly cooked green cabbage.

JOCASTA INNES' ONION, BACON AND POTATO HOTPOT
Serves 4

Jocasta Innes' The Pauper's Cookbook*, first published in 1971 and recently put back in print, was the bible to the cash-strapped of the 70's. 'If I were restricted to cooking the same three recipes for the rest of my life, this would definitely be on the list' she wrote of this hearty hotpot. Here's my slightly modified version.*

50g butter, cut into small squares plus a bit extra for greasing the baking dish or tin
3 tbsp plain flour
568ml (1 pint) milk
2 tbsp (25g) grated cheese
3–4 large Spanish onions, peeled and very thinly sliced
4 large potatoes, peeled and very thinly sliced
125–225g bacon rashers, rind removed and cut into small strips
Salt and pepper

You'll need a small to medium size non-stick saucepan and a large baking dish or roasting tin

Heat the saucepan over a low heat, add the butter and, once it's melted, stir in the flour. Cook for a few seconds, take off the heat and gradually stir in the milk, adding it bit by bit. Bring to the boil, stirring constantly until the sauce is smooth and thick, then turn the heat right down and leave it to simmer. Smother a little of the butter (or some oil) over the base of the baking dish or tin and fill it with alternate layers of sliced onions, sliced potatoes and bacon strips, ending with a layer of potato. Stir the cheese into the sauce, season with salt and pepper and pour it over the potato and onion. Give the dish a good shake to distribute the sauce evenly. Cover the dish with lightly buttered or oiled foil and bake in the oven for 1 hour. Reduce the heat to 180C/350F/Gas 4, uncover the casserole and cook for about another 30–45 minutes until the potatoes are tender and the top browned. Serve with lightly cooked cabbage, greens or a salad.

SPANISH ONIONS?
Not literally Spanish but extra large mild onions. If they're really gigantic you'll probably only need three.

Soup never sounds that substantial but if it's practically thick enough to stand a spoon in, it makes a really satisfying meal with some good crusty bread.

COUNTRY BEAN AND BACON SOUP Serves 4

Mixed, dried pulses such as beans, peas, barley and lentils may not sound madly exciting but they're unbelievably cheap and make brilliant soup, which you can adapt depending on what veg are available. You do need to soak them a day ahead, though. I've kept the seasoning fairly plain on this (for a change!) but have suggested ways you can vary it, or jazz up any leftovers.

125g mixed, dried pulses – often sold as 'country soup mix' – or a 400g tin of mixed beans (see opposite)

2 tbsp vegetable or other oil

2–3 rashers back bacon or 4–6 rashers streaky (preferably smoked), rind removed and chopped into small pieces

1 large onion, peeled and roughly chopped or a couple of leeks, trimmed, washed and finely sliced

2 medium or 1 large carrot, peeled and sliced

2 sticks of celery (optional)

800ml vegetable stock made with 1 tbsp vegetable bouillon powder

3 handfuls shredded spring greens or green cabbage (see note opposite) or 3 tbsp parsley

Ground black pepper

Grated Cheddar, Lancashire or Parmesan cheese to serve if you fancy it

Soak the mixed pulses overnight. Drain them, put them in a saucepan and cover them with fresh cold water. Bring to the boil, spooning off any froth that forms on the surface and boil fast for 10 minutes. Turn the heat down, cover the pan and simmer for another 40–50 minutes until the pulses are cooked. While they're cooking heat the oil in another pan and add the chopped bacon and onion. Fry for about 5 minutes until any liquid has evaporated and they are beginning to brown. Add the sliced carrots and celery, if using, cover the pan and cook on a low heat for 10 minutes. Pour in the stock and continue cooking until the vegetables are soft (about another 20 minutes). Once the pulses are cooked drain them in a sieve or colander. Add the drained pulses and the greens to the cooked vegetables, turn up the heat and bring to the boil again. Simmer for about 3 minutes until the greens are cooked, adding a little extra water or stock if necessary. Season with pepper (there should be enough salt in the stock and the bacon) and serve with crusty bread. You could add some grated cheese but I'm not sure it needs it. (A drizzle of olive oil, Portuguese style, over each bowl is good though.)

GO GREEN!

Spring greens or cabbage can be used instead of parsley. Greens come in loose clusters called a 'head'. Strip the leaves off the stem, wash them and remove any damaged leaves then cut away the tough central rib of the leaf with a sharp knife. Roll up each leaf and slice thinly to give long ribbons of greens. If you're cutting up a cabbage, just remove the central core and slice thinly.

QUICK BEANS

If you haven't got time to soak and boil the bean mix you could use a 400g tin of mixed beans, drained and rinsed. Add it once the veg are cooked.

£ BULK IT OUT

You could make this even more substantial by adding a Polish style boiling sausage when you add the pulses. Cut into chunks when you serve up.

TRY THIS TOO...

• To make the soup more Italian in style you could add a couple of crushed cloves of garlic after you've cooked the onions and bacon and half a tin of tomatoes, or 3–4 fresh tomatoes, skinned and chopped or some passata. Or mix a tablespoon of tomato paste with 2–3 tablespoons of hot water or stock and stir it in.

• You could spice it up by adding garlic and tomato as above and 1 tablespoon of Moroccan Spice Mix (p19) and some fresh coriander (yes, I know I recommend this for everything but it's so good!).

• For a veggie version replace the bacon with smoked tofu. See also the Seasonal Soups on pp46–47.

TUNACO FISH SOUP
Serves 4–6

This spicy south American fish soup is a real winner when you want to show off a bit. I've adapted it from an old American cookbook called *South American Cooking* by Barbara Karoff. (It originally comes from Tunaco, a city on Colombia's Pacific coast.) Cod steaks may sound an extravagant way of buying fish but they have the advantage of having no skin or bones (see p56). If you've got a good fishmonger nearby he may be able to do you a deal on something cheaper though, like hoki or huss.

4 x frozen cod or coley steaks, thawed or about 400g of any thick chunky fish
Juice of 2 limes (about 4 tbsp)
3 tbsp olive oil or vegetable oil
2 medium onions, peeled and coarsely chopped
2 sticks of celery, trimmed and sliced (optional)
2 cloves of garlic, peeled and crushed
750ml vegetable stock made with 1 tbsp vegetable bouillon powder
3 medium-sized potatoes, scrubbed clean and cut into small cubes or 400g sweet potatoes (see below)
4–5 large ripe tomatoes (about 600g) skinned and roughly chopped
4 pickled green chillies, thinly sliced, or 75g sliced jalepeno chillies, or a good slosh of hot chilli sauce
1/2 x 400ml tin coconut milk or 200ml coconut milk made up from coconut powder
A large handful of fresh coriander, washed, stalks removed and roughly chopped
Salt and pepper

Cut each of the cod steaks into 8 pieces. Place in a dish, sprinkle with salt and pour over half the lime juice. Mix together and set aside. Pour the oil into a large saucepan or casserole, add the chopped onion, celery and garlic, stir, put on a lid and cook over a low heat for about 10–15 minutes until the vegetables are soft. Meanwhile, bring the stock to the boil and add the potatoes. Simmer until just cooked (about 10 minutes), and then remove from the heat (if you are using sweet potatoes you don't have to boil them first). Add the chopped tomatoes and sliced chillies to the vegetables, turn up the heat and cook for 3–4 minutes. Pour in the hot stock and potato, bring back to the boil then add the fish and cook for about 5 minutes until the fish is just cooked. Pour the coconut milk into the soup, heat through, then stir in the chopped coriander and the rest of the lime juice. Season with salt and pepper.

PICKLED CHILLIES

You can buy pickled chillies in jars. They've got a less fiery taste than raw chillies. The Spanish ones are particularly good.

TINNED COCONUT MILK

When you open a tin of coconut milk give it a good stir to make it smooth and pourable.

WHY NOT ADD...

• A few frozen prawns.
• Corn cut from the cob (or even frozen corn will do).

£ WHAT TO DO WITH THE REST OF THE CHILLIES...

MAKE MEXICAN-STYLE QUESADILLAS

To make enough for 4 you need a pack of soft flour tortillas. Grate 200g of white crumbly cheese such as Caerphilly and mix in some finely chopped pickled chillies and some crushed garlic (if you can't contemplate anything without garlic). Mash all together with a little milk to make a spreadable consistency. Heat a little oil in a frying pan place a tortilla in the pan and spread a spoonful of the cheese mixture over half the surface. Fold over the other half to make a half-moon shape, press down well then flip the quesadilla over until both sides are well browned and the cheese nice and gooey. Repeat with the remaining tortillas.

£ WHAT TO DO WITH THE REST OF THE COCONUT MILK...

Make the Thai Green Fish Curry on p57, or whiz up with plain yoghurt and fresh ripe mango for a Mango Smoothie (p79).

It's worth occasionally breaking out of the rice and pasta rut to try some other cheap, filling carbs. Here are two great veggie dishes.

BUTTERNUT SQUASH AND RED PEPPER BARLOTTO 🍁 Serves 4–6

Barlotto – a budget risotto made with pearl barley rather than rice – was one of the most popular recipes in my first Beyond Baked Beans *book. Here's a new version based on butternut squash.*

3 tbsp sunflower or light olive oil
1 medium-sized butternut squash (about 600–700g), peeled, de-seeded and cut into small chunks (see below)
2 large red peppers, de-seeded and cut into squares, the same size as the butternut squash
1 medium onion, peeled and roughly chopped
250g pearl barley
1 clove of garlic, peeled and crushed or finely chopped
1/4 tsp turmeric (optional)
2 ripe tomatoes, skinned and chopped or 1/2 a 400g tin of tomatoes, chopped or 200ml passata or 1 tbsp tomato paste
600–700ml vegetable stock made with 1 tbsp vegetable bouillon powder
3 tbsp finely chopped fresh parsley (optional)
Freshly grated Parmesan, Grana Padano or Cheddar to serve
Salt and ground black pepper

Heat the oil in a wok or large saucepan and tip in the cubed squash, peppers and onion. Stir and cook over a medium heat for about 10–15 minutes until the vegetables are beginning to brown and soften. Meanwhile, put the barley in another pan, cover with cold water, bring to the boil, drain and rinse with cold water. Add the garlic and turmeric, if using, to the vegetables in the wok. Stir, add the tomatoes, passata or tomato paste and cook for another couple of minutes. Add the barley, pour in 600ml of the stock, stir and bring to the boil.

Turn the heat down and cover the pan with a lid, or a piece of foil tucked round the edges. Cook for about 30 minutes, adding a little more stock if the barlotto appears to be sticking or getting too thick and gluey. Check to make sure the grains and veg are cooked then season with salt and pepper and stir in the parsley, if you have some. Serve in bowls with grated Parmesan, Grana Padano or Cheddar.

TO PREPARE THE SQUASH

Wipe clean and cut it lengthways into quarters. (You'll need a large sharp knife for this – the skin is tough.) Scoop out the seeds with the tip of a spoon then cut each piece across into 3 or 4 big chunks. Cut the skin off each chunk (easiest if you lay each piece on a chopping board and slice downwards), and then cut into smaller pieces.

COUSCOUS ❁ Serves 6–8

The word couscous refers both to the dish and the grain. This isn't a quick recipe but feeds a lot of people cheaply. Just vary the veg depending on what's in season.

1–1½ kilos mixed veg – say 2–3 carrots, 1–2 parsnips, ½ a swede or a couple of turnips, a small cauliflower and 1–2 courgettes

3 tbsp olive, sunflower or vegetable oil

2 medium onions, peeled and sliced

2 level tbsp Moroccan Spice Mix (see p19)

1½ litres weak vegetable stock made with 1½ tbsp Marigold vegetable bouillon powder or a vegetable stock cube

500g instant couscous

½ a 400g tin of tomatoes or 3 fresh tomatoes, skinned and chopped

1 x 400g tin of chickpeas, drained and rinsed

4 heaped tbsp chopped, fresh coriander

Salt and lemon juice to taste

Chilli sauce to serve (optional)

First get all your veg ready and chopped into even-sized chunks. Put them in piles depending on how long they will take to cook (root veg take longer than other veg, courgettes take the least time). Heat the oil in a large saucepan or casserole and add the onions. Cook over a moderate heat for about 5 minutes then stir in the spices. Cook for a minute then add the stock. Bring to the boil, add the carrots, parsnip and swede, bring back to the boil and simmer for about 7–8 minutes. Add the cauliflower, bring back to the boil and cook for another 5 minutes, then add the sliced courgette. Spoon off about 300ml of the cooking liquid with a ladle or mug, pour it into a bowl and add enough boiling water to bring it up to the amount you need for cooking the couscous (check the packet). Pour the stock over the couscous and leave for 5 minutes for it to absorb. Meanwhile, add the chopped tomatoes, chickpeas and coriander to the vegetables, heat through and leave to simmer for about 5 minutes. Check the seasoning, adding salt and fresh lemon juice to taste. Fork through the couscous to fluff it up then serve in bowls with the vegetables spooned over the top. Offer chilli sauce or harissa diluted with a little of the broth for those who like it hotter.

WHAT'S HARISSA?

Harissa is a spicy, North African chilli-based paste you can buy in ethnic shops.

£ LEFTOVERS?

Leftover couscous grain makes a good salad (see p87).

If you're on a budget you don't need to have a whole lot of different spices or use expensive jars of cook-in sauce. A simple jar of curry paste will spice things up and will last for weeks.

BIG VEGGIE CURRY
🍃 Serves 4–6

Like the couscous on the previous page, this is a totally flexible recipe you can adapt depending on what's available. You just need to make sure all the veg are cooked properly – some take longer than others. If you want to reduce the amounts to serve one, it's easiest to base it on one of those mixed bags of microwaveable vegetables that can often be found reduced.

About 1kg mixed veg which could include: 1 medium onion, peeled and roughly chopped, 1 large carrot, peeled and sliced, $1/2$ a medium cauliflower, cut into florets, 1 small to medium-sized aubergine, cut into cubes, $1/3$ to a $1/2$ butternut squash, peeled, de-seeded and cut into chunks, a handful of green beans, a courgette, trimmed and cut into rounds
4 tbsp vegetable oil
2–3 cloves of garlic, peeled and crushed
2–3 tbsp curry paste, depending how strong the paste is and how hot you want the curry
$1/2$ –1 x 400g tin of tomatoes, roughly chopped
Up to 600ml vegetable stock made with a vegetable stock cube or 1 tbsp vegetable bouillon powder
1 x 400g tin chickpeas (leave out if you're serving a dal alongside)
3 tbsp chopped fresh coriander – optional but good
Salt and lemon juice to taste
Plain yoghurt to serve

Put the harder root veg (see opposite) in a saucepan and cover with boiling water. Bring to the boil and cook for about 10 minutes (adding the cauliflower and beans, if using, half way through). Meanwhile, heat the oil in a wok and stir-fry the aubergine and squash for 3–4 minutes. Add the chopped onion and courgette, turn down the heat a bit and keep frying until the vegetables are soft (about another 5 minutes). Stir in the curry paste and tomatoes then pour in the boiled veg and their cooking water and enough extra stock to cover all the vegetables. Bring to the boil, cover the wok and simmer until the vegetables are tender (about another 10–15 minutes). Add the chickpeas, and coriander if using, and heat through. Check the seasoning, adding salt and lemon juice to taste. Serve with rice, naan or pitta bread and onion raita (p115) or a dollop of plain or soy yoghurt.

• Root veg such as potatoes, sweet potatoes, carrots, swede, turnip and parsnip take longest to cook and should be boiled, steamed or microwaved for 5–10 minutes (depending on size) before adding them to the curry. The smaller you cut them, obviously the less time they'll take. Aubergines, squash, tomato and courgettes are veg with a high water content and are best fried. Frozen peas can be chucked in during the last 2–3 minutes of the cooking time along with the fresh coriander, if using.

QUICK CHICKEN MAKHANI Serves 4–6

Good cook-in sauces are expensive so here's how to make a very easy one of your own. Don't be alarmed at the use of butter and cream – it's authentic!

2 tbsp medium-hot curry paste (I used Patak's Biryani paste)
1–2 cloves of garlic, peeled and crushed
250ml passata or creamed tomatoes
125ml chicken or vegetable stock made with 1/2 stock cube or 2 tsp vegetable bouillon powder
25g butter, cut into cubes
6 skinless, boneless chicken thighs – or 4 breasts (about 500–600g in total), cubed
5–6 tbsp double cream
Salt, ground black pepper and a squeeze of lemon juice
2–3 tbsp finely chopped fresh coriander if you have some

Spoon the curry paste into a saucepan, add the crushed garlic, passata and stock and mix thoroughly. Add the butter and heat gently until it melts then bring the sauce to the boil and add the cubed chicken. Stir well then turn the heat down and simmer for about 10 minutes until the chicken is thoroughly cooked. Stir in the cream and season to taste with salt, pepper and lemon juice. Stir in some fresh coriander if you have some. Serve with rice (see p86).

CARROT DAL 🌱
Serves 4–6

Carrots are a great addition to a dal, giving it a crunchier texture and, of course, making it healthier too. This goes well with the veggie curry on the previous page or, with the Cauliflower and Potato Curry on p63. It's a good cheap meal on its own, or served with chapattis and raita as well.

250g red lentils
1/2 tsp turmeric or extra curry paste
4 cloves of garlic, peeled
1 tbsp vegetable bouillon powder or a vegetable stock cube
3 tbsp sunflower or vegetable oil
1 medium to large onion, peeled and roughly chopped
2–3 carrots, peeled and coarsely grated (about 200g)
1 tsp curry paste or powder
Salt and lemon juice to taste
3 tbsp finely chopped coriander

Put the lentils in a pan with the turmeric, if using, or an extra 1/2 tsp curry paste or curry powder. Add two whole cloves of garlic. Dissolve the vegetable bouillon powder or stock cube with a little boiling water then top up with cold water to the 850ml mark on a measuring jug. Pour over the lentils, stir and bring to the boil, carefully spooning off any froth that rises to the surface. Part cover the pan and simmer for about 25–30 minutes or until the water is absorbed (you want it sloppy rather than stiff). Meanwhile, fry the onion in the oil over a moderate to high heat until they begin to brown (about 5–6 minutes). Turn the heat down and add the grated carrot, the curry paste or powder and the remaining two cloves of garlic, crushed. Mix well and cook over a low heat for about 5 minutes until the carrot is soft. When the lentils are cooked, tip in the carrot mixture and mix thoroughly together. Season the dal with salt and lemon juice to taste, stir in the fresh coriander and leave for 5 minutes before serving.

• See the menu planner on p27 for what to do with any leftovers.

CHAPATTIS 🌱 Serves 4

Chapattis have to be the easiest bread in the world to make. This isn't a totally authentic recipe but it's one of the simplest. I've adapted it from one in Das Sreedharan's book The New Tastes of India.

100g each wholemeal flour and plain flour, or 200g wholemeal flour
1/4 tsp salt
1 tsp cumin seeds (optional)
2 tsp sunflower or vegetable oil plus extra oil for frying

Put the flour, salt and cumin seeds, if using, in a large bowl, mix well and make a hollow in the centre. Pour in 2 teaspoons of oil and about 100ml of water and mix together with a wooden spoon. Using your hand to pull the mixture together to form a dough, adding a little extra water if you need it. Leave the dough for 10 minutes then knead it lightly for 3 minutes on a floured work surface, pushing it away from you with the heel of your hand and using your fingers to bring the far edge towards you. Turn and repeat the action. Divide the dough into 8, roll each piece between your palms then roll it out as thinly as possible with a small rolling pin. Heat a frying pan for 2–3 minutes then add 1/2 tsp of oil and swirl it around the pan. Place a chapatti in the pan and quickly flip it over to the other side, pressing it down well with a spatula. Flip it every few seconds then transfer to a plate lined with a clean tea towel. Cover the chapatti so it doesn't get cold and repeat with the remaining balls of dough, adding a little oil in between each chapatti. (You can cook the chapattis without oil if you prefer. Just press them down into a dry pan.) Serve warm.

SMALL ROLLING PINS

Great for rolling bread – you can buy these in Indian or Pakistani shops.

FRESH CORIANDER CHUTNEY ❦ Serves 4–6

Great with dal or any kind of Indian snack food such as pakoras (p63).

1/2 a large bunch of coriander (about 75g)
2–3 sprigs of mint
300ml (2/3 of a large carton or 2 small cartons) low-fat yoghurt
1 clove of garlic, peeled and crushed
1 green chilli, de-seeded and finely chopped (optional)
1–2 tsp fresh lemon juice
A pinch of ground cumin (optional)
Salt

Wash the coriander thoroughly, shake dry then chop off the thicker stalks. Chop the leaves as finely as possible. Wash the mint, strip the leaves from the stalks and chop very finely too. Put the yoghurt in a bowl and mix in the coriander, mint, crushed garlic and chilli, if using. Season to taste with salt, lemon juice and a little cumin, if you have some. Cover and leave in the fridge for half an hour to let the flavours infuse. Eat within 2 hours of making.

HOW TO STORE FRESH CORIANDER

If you buy coriander that still has its roots put it in a tall glass of water, cover it with a plastic bag, secure the bag with a rubber band and put it in the door of the fridge. It will keep for 4–6 days if you replace the water every couple of days. Cut off what you need and wash it before using.

EASY ONION RAITA ❦ Serves 4–6

300ml (2/3 of a large carton or 2 small cartons) low-fat yoghurt
1 medium onion, peeled and finely sliced
Salt

Tip the yoghurt into a bowl, add the onion, stir well, and season to taste with salt. Leave 15 minutes for the flavours to infuse.

Mezze – the Middle-Eastern word for a selection of shared appetisers – is a great way to eat in the summer when it's too hot for hearty stews. You can put it together entirely from ingredients you buy in, such as hummus, taramasalata, stuffed vine leaves and olives, but that makes it expensive and it's really easy to make a few inexpensive dips and salads of your own.

HOME MADE HUMMUS
☘ Serves 6–8

You might think it crazy to make your own hummus when it's so easily available ready-made but if you're feeding a crowd or want to make enough to last a week, making it yourself is much, much cheaper. You'll need to soak the chickpeas a day ahead, and you'll need a hand-held blender or a food processor. This recipe comes from my book, The Healthy Lunchbox.

125g dried chickpeas
2–3 large cloves of garlic, peeled
3 tbsp tahini paste (stir well before you measure it out)
2 tbsp plain, unsweetened yoghurt (optional – see below)
3–4 tbsp lemon juice
1/2 tsp ground cumin
1/2 tsp salt

Put the chickpeas in a bowl cover with cold water and leave them to soak for at least 12 hours. The next day discard the water and rinse the chickpeas then put them in a saucepan of fresh cold water. Bring them to the boil, skim off any froth, add 2 cloves of garlic (but no salt) and boil them for about 1 1/2–2 hours, topping up the water as necessary, until the skins begin to come away and they are soft enough to squish between your fingers. Turn off the heat and leave them to cool in the pan. Once they are cold, drain the chickpeas, reserving the cooking water and put them in a food processor or blender (or return them to the saucepan if you have a hand-held blender). Start to process them, adding enough of the cooking liquid to keep the mixture moving until you have a thick paste. Add the tahini paste, yoghurt, if using, 3 tablespoons of lemon juice, cumin and salt and whizz together until smooth. (If you want it more garlicky just add one more crushed clove.) Check the seasoning, adding more lemon juice if you think it needs it and some chopped coriander if you like and are eating it straight away.

MAKE THIS DAIRY-FREE
Substitute the chickpea cooking liquor for the yoghurt. You may then want to adjust the seasoning.

TURN IT RED
You could whizz up 2 chopped roasted red peppers (see p64) with the chickpea paste to make a red pepper hummus. Replace the tahini with olive or sunflower oil, reduce the amount of lemon juice slightly and add a pinch of paprika.

RED PEPPER AND 'FAKE FETA' DIP ✤

A good thing to make when you've made a batch of roasted red peppers (see p64).

Whizz up the equivalent of 3 roasted peppers and their oil with about 150–200g crumbled white cheese like Caerphilly or Wensleydale (cheaper than feta). Season with salt, a good squeeze of lemon and a pinch of paprika or a dash of hot pepper sauce.

SERVING PITTA

You've probably discovered this already, but pitta bread tastes immeasurably better if you warm it through before you serve it. It freshens the bread and puffs it up. The easiest way to do it is to pop the breads in the toaster on a low to medium setting, but you can heat them in a dry frying pan, under a grill or in the oven (though that's slow and expensive unless you have it on anyway). Cut it into strips if serving it with a dip. Halve and open each 'pouch' up to fill with a sandwich filling.

BEETROOT, YOGHURT AND CUMIN SALAD
🌱 Serves 4–6

Don't use bottled beetroot in vinegar for this; buy those very good value vacuum-packed packs of beetroot you find in the fruit and veg section of the supermarket.

For the dressing
1/2 tsp Dijon mustard
1 tbsp wine vinegar
3 tbsp sunflower or olive oil
2 heaped tbsp plain yoghurt
Salt and ground black pepper

For the salad
A small pack of cooked beetroot (250–300g), drained and cut into small cubes
2–3 spring onions, trimmed and finely sliced
1 tsp roasted cumin seeds or a pinch of cumin powder

First make the dressing: put the mustard, wine vinegar and seasoning in a bowl and whisk with a fork. Gradually add the oil till you have a thick dressing then mix in the yoghurt. Add the cubed beetroot and spring onion and mix together lightly. Sprinkle with roast cumin seeds or a pinch of cumin powder.

£ LEFTOVER BEETROOT?
If you have any beetroot left over you could add some chopped beetroot to the Corned Beef Hash (p85) to turn it into a Red Flannel Hash (true – that's what it's called!).

TO ROAST CUMIN
Tip the seeds into a dry frying pan and heat over a low to moderate heat, shaking the pan occasionally. Once the seeds begin to release their fragrance and change colour, remove the pan from the heat and cool.

GREEN BEAN AND TOMATO SALAD 🌱
Serves 4–6

Cooked beans and tomatoes go really well together.

300–350g green beans, trimmed and sliced, if they're large
3 tbsp sunflower or olive oil
1 medium onion, peeled and finely chopped
1 clove of garlic
1/2 tsp ground cumin or 1/4 tsp cinnamon
1 tsp tomato paste (if using fresh tomatoes)
4–5 ripe tomatoes, skinned and chopped or 1 x 400g tin of whole tomatoes
Salt

Put the beans in a saucepan, cover with boiling water and bring to the boil. Cook until just tender – about 5–6 minutes. Drain, reserving a little of the cooking water and rinse under cold water. Heat the oil in a frying pan over a moderate heat and add the onion, stir and cook for about 5–6 minutes until beginning to soften and brown. Add the crushed garlic, cumin or cinnamon and tomato paste (if using fresh tomatoes) and stir. Tip in the tomatoes, bring to the boil and simmer for 5 or 6 minutes until the mixture thickens. Tip in the green beans and carry on cooking for another 5 minutes, adding a little of the bean cooking water if the mixture gets too dry. Season with salt to taste and cool. Serve at room temperature with other mezze.

CHARRED AUBERGINE AND TOMATO SALAD
Serves 4–6

Sounds odd. Tastes delicious!

2 medium or 1 large aubergine (about 500g)
4 tbsp olive oil
1 medium onion (about 100g), peeled and roughly chopped
1 clove of garlic, peeled and crushed
2 medium tomatoes, skinned, de-seeded and diced
2 tbsp finely chopped parsley or fresh coriander
1 tbsp finely chopped fresh mint leaves (optional but good)
1–1½ tbsp lemon juice
1 tsp ground cumin
Salt and pepper

Cut the stalks off each aubergine, cut in half lengthways then cut into cubes. Heat a wok for about 2 minutes over a high heat, add the oil, heat for a few seconds and then tip in the aubergine cubes. Stir-fry over a moderate heat for about 5 minutes until lightly browned then turn the heat down low, add the onion and garlic, stir, cover the pan and cook gently for a further 15 minutes, stirring from time to time. Tip the aubergine into a shallow dish while you prepare the other ingredients. When the aubergine is cool (about 20 minutes), cut it up roughly with a knife and fork, then mix in the chopped tomato, parsley, coriander, and mint if using. Season with the lemon juice, cumin, salt and pepper. Serve with pitta bread.

MORE MEZZE
Other dishes that make good mezze: Arab Salad (p61), Tzatziki (p60).

SPOIL YOURSELF

Just because you're on a budget doesn't mean you can't indulge yourself occasionally. But that needn't mean the kind of high calorie blow-out we usually associate with comfort eating. If you can afford a takeaway pizza or a bucket of KFC you can afford steak or salmon for supper, or perhaps some gorgeous fresh fruit. It's just a question of thinking of spoiling yourself in a different way....
Treat your body. Give it a break!

You may also want to spoil someone else of course and here are some seriously impressive, but still relatively inexpensive, recipes to try. Ever cooked duck, made a soufflé or rustled up a Prawn and Avocado Martini (aka prawn cocktail)? It's truly not that difficult.

Just in case you think this section's in danger of getting preachy – relax. If you fancy some toasted waffles with bananas, vanilla ice cream and yummy toffee sauce or some squidgy chocolate pudding (thought so!) there are recipes for those too. Read on....

If you don't want to cook there are plenty of treats around that require little or no effort at all.

6 STARTERS OR INDULGENT SNACKS

PATE AND TOAST

French food isn't that fashionable currently so paté is cheap. Serve with toast, a few cornichons (small pickled cucumbers) or onion marmalade (see p65) and maybe a few lightly dressed salad leaves if you're feeling flashy.

FISH PATE AND TOAST

Smoked mackerel, smoked salmon and crab paté are all bargain buys. Scoop out of their unglamorous plastic containers and serve with wholemeal toast, a few salad leaves and a wedge of lemon.

READY-MADE FRESH SOUPS

Again it's just a question of tarting them up. A squeeze of lemon, a swirl of cream or yoghurt and a sprinkling of fresh herbs can work wonders. Everybody does it, darling.

FRESH ASPARAGUS ♥

A fantastic treat when in season (May – June). Cut the spears about two thirds of the way down from the tip and rinse with cold water. Put them in a steamer or microwaveable dish with 3tbsp water, cover with a damp sheet of kitchen towel and cook for about 3–4 minutes until just tender. Serve hot, dunked into a hot lemon butter dip (50g of melted butter with 2 tbsp lemon juice) or, after cooking, refresh with cold water to preserve the colour, pat dry and serve with a drizzle of vinaigrette and a little crumbled goats' cheese (see p126). (Don't chuck away the end of the spears, save them for a pasta sauce or a soup.)

GOOD ITALIAN DRIED EGG PASTA

Cook following the instructions on the packet and serve with loads of butter and freshly grated Parmesan cheese. Allow about 75g a head for a starter or snack.

BAKED CAMEMBERT ♥

Cheat's fondue! Buy a Camembert in a wooden box, remove any plastic wrapping and replace it in its box. Rub a halved clove of garlic over the surface of the cheese and trickle over a spoonful of oil. Replace the lid of the box and bake in a hot oven (200 C/400 F/Gas 6) for about 15 minutes. Serve with crusty bread or breadsticks to dunk in the gooey cheese. Enough for 2.

SMOKED SALMON

Smoked salmon, like salmon, is often on offer, especially around celebrations like Christmas and Valentine's Day. You may have to buy a slightly bigger pack than you need to get the deal, but let's face it – it's easy enough to eat up the leftovers.

SMOKED SALMON PIZZA

One of my all time favourite flash recipes. Simple but stunning.

1 1/2 tbsp olive oil
1 ready-to-cook thin, plain pizza base
125g cream cheese
1 1/2 tbsp milk
2 tsp onion, very finely chopped (optional but good)
A small (125g) pack of wafer-thin smoked salmon or, ordinary sliced smoked salmon
A quarter of a lemon or about 2 tsp lemon juice
1/2 a small bag of rocket
Ground black pepper

Lightly brush or smear the top of the pizza base with oil. Cook for about a minute each side under a moderate grill until crisp but still soft. Set aside on a rack and cool for 15 minutes. Turn the cream cheese into a bowl and mash up with the milk so you get a soft, spreading consistency. Add the chopped onion, if using, and season with ground pepper (you shouldn't need salt because the salmon will be salty). When the base has cooled down spread it with the cream cheese mixture then drape the smoked salmon pieces artistically over the top. Squeeze over a little lemon juice and season with black pepper. Scatter a small handful of rocket leaves over the salmon and drizzle over a little extra oil.

BASE NOTE

The best kind of bases to buy are the ones in the pizza section of the supermarket rather than those long-life ones in boxes.

SMOKED SALMON BAGELS

Not as flashy but just as tasty. Warm the bagels through under a grill, split them, spread with the cream cheese mixture above and stuff with smoked salmon. Season with lemon juice and pepper. Particularly good with sweet and sour pickled cucumbers.

PRAWNS

Prawns perfectly exemplify one of the basic rules about budget shopping. The more fashionable something is the more you pay for it. Take tiger prawns. They look much sexier than those tiny pale pink wiggles of North Atlantic prawns but they taste no better – unless you buy them raw (see Gorgeous Garlicky Prawns, opposite). And they cost at least twice as much.

Packs of frozen prawns are a really good budget-buy especially when they're on special offer. You really don't need that many and they do add a touch of glamour to an otherwise basic dish (see also Spaghetti Marinara, p38; Courgette and Prawn Couscous Salad, p87; Prawns and Mayo baked potato topping, p103; Tunaco Fish Soup, p108).

PRAWN AND AVOCADO MARTINIS Serves 2

Aka prawn cocktail. Martinis sounds much cooler, though.

125g small North Atlantic
  prawns, fresh or thawed
  frozen
1 ripe avocado
1 tbsp lemon juice
A handful of finely shredded
  iceberg or little gem lettuce

For the dressing
2 tbsp mayonnaise
2 tbsp low-fat yoghurt
1–1 1/2 tsp tomato ketchup
  – depending how pink you
  want it
1 small clove of garlic, peeled
  and crushed or, 1 spring
  onion, trimmed and finely
  sliced (optional)
1/2 tsp Thai fish sauce (optional
  but adds an edge)
Salt, pepper and hot pepper
  sauce if you have some
1 tbsp finely chopped parsley,
  or fresh coriander plus a little
  extra for decoration
**You'll need two large martini
  glasses or other stemmed
  glasses**

First make the dressing. Mix together the mayo, yoghurt, ketchup and garlic or onion. Add the Thai fish sauce, if using, and season with salt, pepper and a few drops of hot pepper sauce if you like. You could add a squeeze of lemon too but the avocado will taste quite lemony. Drain any liquid off the prawns, mix them with the dressing and stir in the parsley or coriander. Put the lemon juice in a bowl. Quarter and peel the avocado (see opposite), cut into small cubes and mix with the lemon juice. Put a little shredded lettuce in the bottom of each glass, spoon over half the cubed avocado and top with half the prawns. Decorate with a little extra parsley or coriander and serve straightaway with triangles of brown bread and butter (very retro!).

HOW TO
HANDLE AN AVOCADO

- To tell if an avocado is ripe: press it gently round the narrow end. It should 'give' very slightly.
- The easiest way to halve an avocado is to run a knife round it lengthways, then hold one half in each hand and twist them apart. Scoop out the stone with the end of a knife or spoon, then peel it and cut into chunks.

GORGEOUS GARLICKY
PRAWNS Serves 2

Raw prawns are rather an alarming shade of grey but don't be put off. They really do taste much juicier and sweeter than ones that have been sitting in a plastic pack for several days. You can of course cook more than eight if you're feeling flush, but four each is about right for an indulgent starter. Perfect for Valentine's Day or any other seduction opportunity....

8 large raw prawns with their
   shells on
1 tbsp sunflower or vegetable oil
25g (1 tbsp) soft butter
2 cloves of garlic, peeled and
   crushed
A few chilli flakes or a pinch of
   hot chilli powder (optional)
A good squeeze of lemon juice
A heaped tbsp finely chopped
   parsley (optional)

Have everything ready before you start. Rinse the prawns and pat them dry. Heat a wok, add the oil then add the butter. As soon as the foaming has died down chuck in the prawns, garlic and chilli flakes, if using, and stir-fry for about 2 minutes until the prawns are hot through and have turned completely pink. Add a good squeeze of lemon to the pan, stir in the chopped parsley, if using, and serve with crusty bread.

RINSE OR LICK?

You may want to put a small bowl of water on the table to rinse your fingers in between each prawn. Or you may just want to lick them....

GOATS' CHEESE

If you're not yet converted to the joys of goats' cheese you've a treat in store. It's pricier than cow's cheese, true, but is an affordable indulgence.

GOATS' CHEESE AND THYME SOUFFLE ♨

Don't be put off by the word soufflé. This recipe is truly not that difficult once you've mastered the art of separating eggs and whipping up and folding in whites (see footnotes). I've adapted it from a recipe from one of my favourite chefs, Sally Clarke who in turn got it from the Californian chef Alice Waters. Serves 3–4 as a flashy starter, 2–3 as a main course.

1 tsp soft butter
3 really fresh large free-range eggs, separated
200g fresh soft goats' cheese (without rind)
5 tbsp double cream
4–6 heaped tbsp freshly grated Parmesan (depending on how mature your Parmesan is, if it's extra mature Parmesan use the smaller amount)
1 tsp chopped fresh thyme or ½ tsp dried thyme
Ground black pepper
You'll also need a large shallow ovenproof dish and some electric hand beaters or a rotary whisk

Preheat the oven to 200C/400F/Gas 6. Put a baking sheet on the shelf. Smear the butter over the base and sides of your ovenproof dish. Beat the egg yolks lightly with a wooden spoon then tip in the goats' cheese and beat until smooth (use a fork if you can't get it to break up easily). Add the cream, 2 tablespoons of the Parmesan, the thyme and black pepper and beat again. Beat the egg whites with the whisk until stiff enough to hold their shape when you pull out the beaters. Take a large tablespoon of the whites and fold it into the goats' cheese mixture (see opposite). Then lightly fold in the remaining whites. Tip the mixture into the prepared dish and sprinkle the remaining Parmesan over the top. Put the dish in the oven and bake for 10–15 minutes until puffed up and golden. (Ovens vary so it may even take slightly longer than this.) Serve with crusty bread and a green salad.

TO SEPARATE EGGS

You need a cup and two grease-free bowls. Crack the first egg against the side of the cup and pull the two halves apart letting the white fall into the cup. Tip the yolk carefully from one half of the shell to the other trying not to catch it on the broken shell and letting the rest of the white fall away. Put the yolk in one bowl and the white in another and repeat with the remaining eggs.

TO FOLD IN EGG WHITES

Use a large metal spoon and cut through the mixture, scooping it up repeatedely so the bottom part of the mixture comes to the top. This should be a light, deft movement – you're not beating it like a cake. Don't overmix it – stop as soon as the egg whites are combined with the base mix.

GRILLED GOATS' CHEESE SALAD WITH GARLIC TOASTS 🍁
Serves 4 as a starter or 2 as a main course

Basically a posh version of cheese on toast with a few leaves – but none the worse for that.

4 slices of walnut, wholewheat or sourdough bread from a small loaf
1–2 tbsp sunflower or olive oil
1 clove of garlic, peeled and cut in half
2 x 100g slices goats' cheese 'log'
A small pack of mixed salad leaves
5 tbsp vinaigrette

Pre-heat the grill on a medium setting. Next make the garlic toasts: heat a frying pan or ridged grill pan for 2–3 minutes until hot. Trickle a little oil over each side of the bread you've sliced and rub it in. Place the slices in the pan and cook for about 1 minute on each side until lightly browned. Rub the cut garlic over the surface of the toast and set aside. Carefully slice each piece of goats' cheese log into two. Lay the discs on a lightly oiled piece of foil on the bottom of the grill pan (not on a raised rack – you don't want the cheese right under the heat). Grill until lightly browned and beginning to melt (about 4–5 minutes). Divide the salad leaves between the plates and spoon over the dressing. Lay the grilled goats' cheese slices on top and put a slice of toast alongside.

TO MAKE THE VINAIGRETTE

Put $1/2$ tsp Dijon mustard in a bowl with 1 tbsp wine vinegar. Season with salt and pepper and whisk with a fork. Gradually whisk in 4 tablespoons of oil to produce a thick dressing. Add a few more drops of vinegar if needed.

While not as cheap as chicken, salmon is regularly on special offer, though usually as a BOGOF (buy one, get one free) offer which may mean you have to buy more than you want unless you have a freezer. Fillets are easier to cope with than salmon steaks. If you're planning to fry or grill the fish go for the so-called 'tail' fillet which is more even in thickness than ones cut higher up the fish. It's generally nicer without the skin, though that may make it more expensive.

Salmon is versatile. It can be treated delicately and microwaved or steamed, or handled more robustly and pan-fried, grilled or baked. It's good with a simple butter and lemon sauce but can also handle a tandoori or teriyaki marinade. Here are a couple of other ideas.

Note: before cooking salmon run your fingertips over the fish to see if there are any bones. If there are remove them with tweezers.

THAI-STYLE SALMON WITH SUGAR SNAP PEAS Serves 1

Spoiling yourself doesn't necessarily mean stuffing yourself. Here's a healthy dish that'll make you feel fantastic.

For the dressing
Juice of 1/2 a lime (about 1 1/2 tbsp)
1 tbsp fish sauce (nam pla)
1 tsp wine vinegar
1 tsp caster sugar
1 small clove of garlic, peeled and crushed
1/4 red pepper, de-seeded and finely chopped
1 small chilli, de-seeded and finely chopped (optional)
1 tbsp fresh coriander, roughly chopped

For the salmon and peas
1 tsp oil
1 skinless salmon fillet, about 150g
100g sugar snap peas or mange-tout

First make the dressing: in a bowl mix together the lime juice, fish sauce, wine vinegar and 1 tablespoon of water. Stir in the sugar, garlic, red pepper and chilli, if using. Heat a non-stick frying pan, add the oil and place the salmon in the pan, flat side downwards. Cook for 3–4 minutes then flip it over and cook for another 1–2 minutes. Meanwhile, microwave or steam the mange-tout or sugar snap peas till just done (2–3 minutes). Remove the salmon from the pan and put on a plate. Drain the sugar snap peas, and spoon round the salmon. Pour the dressing into the pan and bubble up for 30 seconds, add the chopped coriander then pour over the salmon and peas.

COOKING SALMON
The difference in the timing reflects the thickness of the salmon. Watch the salmon change colour from deep to pale pink as the heat penetrates it. Once the colour has changed half way through the fillet, flip it over.

PESTO-CRUSTED SALMON WITH RED PEPPER AND AVOCADO SALSA
Serves 4

A flash, but incredibly easy, recipe. There's a lot of salsa but I doubt if you'll have any left over.

1 190g jar of red pesto
2–3 natural dried breadcrumbs (not those bright orange ones)
1 tsp oil
4 x salmon fillets (about 150–175g each)

For the salsa
250g cherry tomatoes, stalks removed and finely chopped
1 bunch of spring onions, trimmed and finely sliced
1 small to medium red pepper, de-seeded and finely chopped
2 small green or red chillies, de-seeded and finely chopped (optional)
6–7 tbsp freshly-squeezed lime juice (about 3 limes) plus 1 whole lime
2 medium-sized ripe avocados
3 tbsp finely chopped coriander
Salt

Preheat the oven to 190C/375F/Gas 5. Mix the pesto with enough breadcrumbs to make a thick but still spreadable consistency (probably 2 tablespoons, maybe a bit more). Lightly grease a roasting tin or baking dish with the oil and lay the salmon fillets in it, skin side down. Spread the pesto paste evenly over the fillets and bake for 15–20 minutes until the salmon is cooked. Meanwhile cut up the ingredients for the salsa, except for the avocado, and mix them together with the lime juice. Once the salmon is cooked, peel and chop the avocado (see p125 for how to stone an avocado) and add to the salsa along with the chopped coriander. Season with salt and mix together lightly. Put a piece of salmon on each plate with a wedge of lime and a good couple of spoonfuls of salsa. You could also serve some new potatoes with this or just lay on a few plain tortilla chips.

Cheap steak is obviously not the most tender steak but it can be made surprisingly tasty. Firstly, it helps to beat it out thinly. You can also marinate it, which will help to improve the flavour. Don't cook it too long – that toughens it – and rest it on a warm plate for at least 3 minutes after you've cooked it to help the meat fibres relax.

ITALIAN-STYLE STEAK
Serves 1

Steak, like salmon, is regularly on special offer and often you can buy just one piece, which makes it an affordable treat for one. Just marinate it and serve Italian-style with a squeeze of lemon.

1 x 200g rump or sirloin steak
1 tbsp olive or sunflower oil plus extra for serving
1 tbsp lemon juice plus extra for serving
1 clove of garlic, peeled and thinly sliced
Salt and ground black pepper

Put the steak on a chopping board and trim off the excess fat around the edge. Place a sheet of Clingfilm or foil over the top and bash with a rolling pin or the side of a tin to tenderise the steak. Mix the oil and lemon juice on a plate or shallow dish and add the sliced garlic. Place the steak in the marinade and turn it over so that both sides are coated with the oil and lemon juice. Cover and leave for at least half an hour. Heat a frying pan until hot (about 2–3 minutes). Take the steak out of the marinade, scraping off the garlic slices and pat dry with kitchen towel. Place the steak in the pan, cook for 1$\frac{1}{2}$ minutes then turn over and cook for another minute. Remove from the pan and set aside on a plate. Lightly cover with foil and leave for 3–4 minutes. Season with salt, pepper, a squeeze of lemon juice and a little extra olive oil. Serve with a salad and sautéed potatoes (see p48). Cook them first and reheat while the steak is resting.

STEAK TIPS
• About 2–3 minutes results in a medium-rare steak. If you want your steak less pink, cook for an extra minute each side.
• The best type of pan to cook a steak in is a ridged cast-iron pan which you can heat till almost smoking. This gives the steak a barbecued effect. You can often find them cheap in charity shops or on offer in supermarkets and hardware stores.

STEAK AND ONIONS
Serves 2

The nearest you can get to a joint of roast beef without breaking the bank.

2 x rump or sirloin steaks, about 200g each
2 tbsp sunflower or vegetable oil
2 medium onions, peeled and thinly sliced
3 tbsp wine vinegar
100ml meat stock made with 1/4 tsp Marmite
A good slice of butter (about 25g)
Salt and pepper

Cut the fat from around the edge of the steak and place on a chopping board. Beat it out thinly as described in the previous recipe. Heat the oil in a frying pan, add the sliced onions and cook over a low heat for about 10–15 minutes until completely soft and lightly browned. Turn the heat up, pour in the wine vinegar and boil until the vinegar has almost evaporated. Add the stock, bubble up then tip the onions into a bowl. Rinse and dry the frying pan and then heat for 2–3 minutes without any oil. Smear the steaks with the remaining oil, then, once the pan is hot, fry the steaks for 1 1/2 minutes each side. Set aside on a plate to rest, lightly covered with foil. Tip the onions back in the pan and heat through adding a little extra water if the sauce is too thick. Stir in the butter, add back any meat juices, season with salt and pepper and serve. Good with mash, baked or roast potatoes and some green beans or peas.

Duck is the new chicken. Well maybe not quite yet, but it's suddenly become much more affordable. Added to which people obviously don't quite know what to do with it so you often find it knocked down in price at the end of the day. Duck breasts are the easiest to cook but likely to be the most expensive. Duck legs on the other hand are great value and can be used in the French bistro-style recipe, opposite.

HONEY ROAST DUCK WITH STIR-FRIED GREENS Serves 2

Honey, soy and duck are a match made in heaven.

1 tbsp clear honey
2 tbsp soy sauce
2 duck breasts
1 head of spring greens or, 1/2 a small green cabbage or a head of broccoli
1 clove of garlic, peeled and crushed
1 tbsp wine vinegar
3–4 tbsp chicken or light vegetable stock made with 1/4 tsp vegetable bouillon powder
Salt

Preheat the oven to 200C/400F/ Gas 6. Spoon the honey into a bowl and add 1 tablespoon of boiling water, 2 tablespoons of soy sauce and a few drops of hot pepper sauce, if you have some. Using a sharp knife, trim any excess fat from around the edges of the duck breasts. Score diagonally across the fat with a sharp knife. Put a small frying pan on the hob without any oil and heat for 2–3 minutes until hot. Place the duck breasts, skin side down and fry for 5 minutes, pressing down with a spatula to make sure the skin browns evenly. Turn the breasts over and brown the other side for 30 seconds. Place the duck, skin side up, in a small roasting tin and smear over the honey and soy marinade. Roast for 10 minutes (rare) 15 minutes (medium rare) or 20 minutes (well done). Meanwhile, pour off all except 1 tablespoon of the duck fat that has accumulated in the frying pan, put back on the heat, add a crushed clove of garlic, stir and add the greens or cabbage. Stir-fry for 2–3 minutes until tender, adding the remaining soy sauce. When the duck has cooked transfer it to a warm plate and cover lightly with foil. Pour the excess fat from the roasting dish and add the vinegar, bubble up for a minute. Pour in the stock and simmer for 5 minutes, then pour in any juices that have accumulated under the duck breasts. Slice the duck breasts thickly and serve with the stir-fried greens and the pan juices. Mashed sweet potato – or ordinary mash – would also go well with this.

ROAST DUCK, SAUSAGE AND GARLICKY BEANS
Serves 4

I've written this gutsy French-inspired recipe for four people but you can easily expand it to feed eight or more. It's basically a deconstructed cassoulet, but a good deal less effort.

4 x duck legs
1 tsp sunflower or vegetable oil
Salt
1 x 400g pack of Toulouse or other garlicky sausages

For the beans
3 tbsp sunflower or olive oil
2 large cloves of garlic, peeled and crushed
2 tsp vegetable bouillon powder
4 tbsp passata or creamed tomatoes or 1 1/2 tbsp tomato paste
2 x 400g tins of butter beans or haricot beans, drained and rinsed
3 tbsp finely chopped fresh parsley
Salt and ground black pepper

Preheat the oven to 200C/400F/Gas 6. Using kitchen scissors or a sharp knife, cut any excess fat from around the edges of the duck pieces and prick the skin of each piece with the prongs of a fork. Coat the base of a large roasting tin with the one teaspoon of oil. Lay the duck pieces in the tin and sprinkle with salt. Cook for 20 minutes and then take the tin out and pour away any fat that has accumulated into a bowl (good for frying potatoes later!). Cut between the sausage links and put the sausages in the roasting tin, turning them over in the fat so that all sides are coated. Return the pan to the oven for another 15 minutes. In the meantime get on with the beans. Heat the oil over a low heat in a large saucepan, add the crushed garlic and stir in the vegetable bouillon powder. Add the passata, creamed tomatoes or tomato paste, stir well and tip in the beans. Add 3 tablespoons of water and cook gently, stirring occasionally, adding more water whenever the beans look like getting dry. Pour the fat off the duck again, turn over the sausages and return the pan to the oven for another 15–20 minutes until both are well browned. Keep the beans on a low heat, occasionally stirring them and adding more water. Stir in the parsley 5 minutes before serving. When the duck and sausages are well browned serve them up with the beans and a green salad.

There are so many incredibly desirable ready-made desserts on offer that you may feel there's little point in making them yourself. The only reason for doing so being that they might be cheaper, taste better, or really wow someone you want to impress. What you can do is make them look classy. Serve shop-bought ice cream with a homemade sauce. Or smother strawberries with fresh raspberry sauce and serve them with homemade meringues. Pretty them up a bit.

TOASTED WAFFLES WITH BANANAS, VANILLA ICE-CREAM AND YUMMY TOFFEE SAUCE ✿ Serves 3–4

Naughty but nice.

3–4 scoops Vanilla ice cream
3–4 waffles
3–4 small bananas
For the sauce
50g butter
4 tbsp light soft brown or
    Demerara sugar
6 tbsp double cream
A small pinch of salt

If your ice cream is not 'soft scoop' take it out of the freezer before you start the sauce so it's easy to spoon when you want to serve it. To make the sauce: put the butter and sugar into a saucepan over a low heat until the butter has melted and the sugar is completely dissolved. Stir in the cream and heat until almost boiling. Simmer for 2–3 minutes then take off the heat and stir. Toast the waffles on a low setting (they'll seem soggy at first and then crisp up) and slice the bananas. Put a waffle on each plate, with a scoop of ice cream alongside, top with sliced banana and pour over the warm sauce.

MANGO, ORANGE AND LIME SALAD ✿
Serves 2–4

As virtuous as the previous recipe is decadent.

1 medium to large ripe mango
Juice of 1 orange (or 4 tbsp
    ready-prepared freshly
    squeezed orange juice)
Juice of 1 lime
Sugar or sugar syrup to taste
Greek yoghurt to serve

Peel and cut up the mango into chunks as described on p79, saving the juice. Mix together the lime and orange juice. Tip the mango chunks and their juice into the fruit juice and mix together well. Sweeten to taste and serve in little glass bowls topped with Greek yoghurt (or ordinary yoghurt mixed with an equal amount of cream).

• Choose mangoes that are ripe but not too ripe, or they'll turn to mush when you cut them. The cheapest place to buy them is from an Indian or Pakistani store.

STRAWBERRIES WITH FRESH RASPBERRY SAUCE 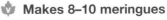 Serves 2

Really only worth making in the summer when strawberries are fully ripe. And cheap.

125g fresh or thawed, frozen
    raspberries
Sugar Syrup to sweeten
    (see p80)
250g ripe strawberries
Double cream to serve

Mash the raspberries with a fork then push the pulp through a sieve with a wooden spoon. Sweeten to taste with sugar syrup. De-stalk the strawberries, cutting away any white unripe fruit around the stalk. Slice into two glass dishes. Pour over the raspberry sauce and serve with cream – and the meringues below, if you feel like making some.

GOLDEN MERINGUES
 Makes 8–10 meringues

If you have any leftover egg whites it's always worth making a batch of meringues. They cost next to nothing and taste truly wonderful. I've adapted the recipe from one of Delia Smith's I've been using for years.

2 large fresh, preferably
    free-range, egg whites (see
    how to separate eggs on p127)
110g golden (unrefined) caster
    sugar

You will need a large bowl, an electric or rotary whisk, a baking sheet and some non-stick baking parchment

Preheat your oven to 150C/300F/Gas 2. Put the egg whites in a large, scrupulously clean bowl (clean because the whites won't beat up properly if there's grease on the surface) and whisk them with a hand-held electric whisk or rotary whisk until stiff. (The whites should hold a peak when you draw the whisk up through them.) Add the sugar a heaped tablespoon at a time, beating the whites well between each addition. It should end up very stiff and shiny. Lay a sheet of baking parchment over the baking tray. Using two dessertspoons (the kind you use for cereal) take spoonfuls of the mixture with one spoon and scoop it out with the other onto the tray – you should get 8–10 meringues. Put the tray in the oven, shut the door then turn down the heat to 140C/275F/Gas 1. Cook for 1–1$\frac{1}{2}$ hours then turn off the oven and leave the meringues to cool in the residual heat until completely cold. You can serve them as they are, or sandwich the halves together with whipped cream.

There's a big economy you can make on chocolate – without sacrificing quality. Buy it from the baking section rather than the confectionery section of the supermarket – it's about half the price of good dark eating chocolate. The kind to look for is described as Belgian Luxury Chocolate and is often sold in 200g packs. So you'll have leftovers to use up. What a shame!

SQUIDGY CHOCOLATE PUDDING
Serves 4 (OK, 2)

This is the most fantastic pudding – a gooey cake with its own chocolate sauce. The original recipe is TV chef Mike Robinson's. I've simplified it slightly.

100g luxury dark Belgian chocolate (see previous note)
100g cubed butter (preferably unsalted) plus extra for greasing the baking dish
3 tbsp caster sugar (preferably unrefined)
2 large fresh, preferably free-range, egg yolks (see p127 for how to separate eggs)
2 large, fresh, preferably free-range, eggs, lightly beaten
2 tsp plain flour
Double cream or vanilla ice cream to serve

You will also need a bowl, a roasting tin and a small, shallow ovenproof baking dish that will hold 500ml of liquid

Put a saucepan of hot water over a very low heat and fit a bowl over the top. Add the chocolate and butter and melt gently. (Don't let the water touch the bowl or boil – it will 'seize' the chocolate and make it impossible to mix.) Take the pan off the heat and beat the chocolate and butter together with a wooden spoon. Stir in the sugar. Add the egg yolks and mix in then the whole eggs. Finally sieve or sprinkle over the flour and mix it in. Lightly grease the base and sides of the baking dish and pour in the chocolate mixture. Transfer to the fridge and leave it for 30 minutes to an hour. Preheat the oven to 180C/350F/Gas 4. Fill a roasting tin with warm water and put the baking dish in the tin. Cook for 20–25 minutes (see opposite) until the top of the pudding is risen and puffy but the middle is still wobbly. Remove the pudding from the oven, leave it to rest for a minute or two, then serve with cream or vanilla ice cream.

CHOCOLATE TIPS

• It's hard to be exact about the cooking time because oven temperatures vary. It could be done in less than 20 minutes. It might take longer. Keep an eye on it – without taking the pudding out of the oven.

• Instead of heating the chocolate and butter over hot water you could microwave them. Follow the instructions in the handbook or the back of the chocolate wrapper.

ULTIMATE CHOCOLATE SAUCE 🍁 Serves 4

Bliss on vanilla ice cream.

100g dark luxury Belgian
　chocolate (see intro opposite)
5 tbsp whipping cream
2–3 tsp of caster sugar
　(optional)

Melt the chocolate and cream in a bowl over hot water as described above. Sweeten to taste with caster sugar, adding 1–2 tablespoons of water to give you a pouring consistency.

CHOCOLATE REFRIGERATOR CAKE
🍁 **Makes 16 pieces – enough for 8... theoretically**

Not really a cake – more a gooey biscuit. Cocoa is another way of getting an intense chocolatey flavour without having to splash out on expensive chocolate.

150g Rich Tea biscuits
175g cubed butter, preferably
　unsalted
4 level tbsp golden syrup
3 level tbsp cocoa powder
75g mixed chopped nuts
100g raisins
1/2 tsp sunflower or vegetable oil

You will need a small, shallow square or rectangular cake tin or baking dish

Put the biscuits into a plastic bag and break up roughly with a rolling pin or the side of a tin (you want a mixture of fine and not-so-fine pieces). Put the butter and syrup into a saucepan and melt over a low heat. Sieve the cocoa powder into the mixture, stir and cook for few seconds. Take off the heat, tip in the biscuits, nuts and raisins and mix well. Lightly oil the baking tin or dish, wiping off any excess with kitchen towel, tip in the 'cake' mixture and press down firmly, smoothing over the surface. Cover with Clingfilm and chill in the fridge for several hours. Before serving, divide the 'cake' into 16 pieces. Prise it out of the tin (easier once you've removed the first piece) and return the remainder to the fridge. Assuming there is a remainder.

SPOONING SYRUP

The easiest way to get a level spoonful of syrup is to dip your spoon into a mug of boiling water before you put it in the tin. That way the syrup won't get stuck on the spoon.

138 MORE BUDGET RECIPES

If you enjoyed the recipes in this book there are many more to try in my other student cookbooks *Beyond Baked Beans* (BBB) and *Beyond Baked Beans Green* (BBBG) including:

EGGS
- Huevos Rancheros ❧ (BBB)
- Parsee-style eggs with potato, spinach and cumin ❧ (BBBG)
- Piperrada ❧ (BBBG)
- Surprisingly good spring onion and beansprout omelette ❧ (BBBG)

PASTA AND RICE
- Broccoli, chilli and garlic pasta ❧ (BBBG)
- Green rice with (or without) broccoli ❧ (BBBG)
- Quick buttered vegetable pasta ❧ (BBBG)
- Penne with courgettes and lemon ❧ (BBB)
- Roast Mediterranean vegetable pasta bake ❧ (BBBG)

SOUPS
- Caramelised Cauliflower soup ❧ (BBBG)
- Carrot and coriander soup ❧ (BBB)
- Chunky potato, onion and garlic soup ❧ (BBB)
- Hot chilli butternut squash soup ❧ (BBB)
- Italian Bean and Pasta Soup ❧ (BBBG)
- Pea, broccoli and mint soup ❧ (BBB)
- Three-can chilli bean soup ❧ (BBB)

MEAT AND FISH
Baked chicken with garlic and lovely lemony potatoes (BBB)
Chicken bruschetta (BBB)
Easy French tuna and bean salad (BBB)
Easy Italian tuna and bean salad (BBB)
Fish fingers three ways (BBB)
Kebda with warm pepper salad (BBB)
Sweet chicken with miracle pepper sauce (BBB)
Sardine tartines (BBB)
Turkey scallopini with lemon, capers and parsley (BBB)
Warm potato and sausage salad (BBB)

VEGGIE MAINS
- Aubergine and pea curry ❀ (BBBG)
- Basque butterbean stew ❀ (BBBG)
- Cheese-crusted veggie shepherd's pie ❀ (BBBG)
- Classic veggie chilli ❀ (BBBG)
- Crispy cheesy garlicky potatoes ❀ (BBBG)
- Harvester's pie ❀ (BBBG)
- Mushroom barlotto ❀ (BBB)
- Portabella mushroom 'steaks' with garlic and parsley butter ❀ (BBB)
- Spiced sweet potato, pepper and aubergine bake ❀ (BBB)

VEGGIE SIDES AND SALADS
- Carrot and lentil pilau ❀ (BBBG)
- Cheese, celery and apple salad with yoghurt and honey dressing ❀ (BBB + BBBG)
- GMVs (Grilled Mediterranean Vegetables) ❀ (BBBG)
- Greek(ish) salad ❀ (BBB)
- Half-baked potatoes ❀ (BBBG)
- Rosti ❀ (BBBG)
- Thai green apple salad ❀ (BBBG)
- Warm broad bean and mint salad with chickpea and cumin pancakes ❀ (BBBG)

DIPS AND RELISHES
- Authentic rough-crushed guacamole ❀ (BBB)
- Black eye bean salsa ❀ (BBBG)
- Easy roast red pepper hummus ❀ (BBBG)
- Red hot pineapple salsa ❀ (BBB)

SWEETS AND TREATS
- American breakfast pancakes with blueberries (BBB)
- Apple crumble (BBB)
- Chocolate-dipped strawberries (BBBG)
- Crunchy lemon pancakes (BBB)
- Fruit couscous (BBBG)
- Pink coconut rice (BBBG)
- Roast cinnamon peaches with Greek yoghurt and honey (BBB)
- Simple, brilliant chocolate mousse (BBBG)
- Sugared plum toasts (BBBG)
- Warm chocolate chip cookies (BBB)

WWW.BEYONDBAKEDBEANS.COM

The website, which was listed by the *Independent* in its top 50 websites for foodies and among the 8 best for 'recipes, chat and reference'. If you want to contribute a recipe or share a tip e-mail **fiona@beyondbakedbeans.com**.

144 ACKNOWLEDGEMENTS

THANKS TO...

Many thanks to all the human guinea pigs who have braved these breadline meals, especially my husband Trevor and kids Will, Jo, Kate and Flyn who have all been diplomatic enough to say they enjoyed them. (They know what's good for them!) Thanks too to the long-suffering editorial team at my publisher Absolute Press – Jon, Meg and Matt (we got there eventually...) and to Andy for his usual brilliant, funky designs. Finally, thanks to Kerry Torrens, who contributes to the website www.beyondbakedbeans.com for keeping me on the nutritional straight and narrow.

ABOUT THE AUTHOR

Fiona Beckett has been a student (twice) and has also been on the receiving end of endless calls from her four children – which still go on now – about how to cook everthing from cheese on toast to risotto. She's also an award-winning journalist who has written for most of the national press, from the *People* to the *Financial Times*. She currently writes on food and drink for *Sainsbury's Magazine*, is contributing editor to the wine magazine *Decanter* and runs two websites, including the website of this book, www.beyondbakedbeans.com. All of which leaves not nearly enough time to spend with her long-suffering friends and family or following the fortunes of Liverpool Football Club.